T0159128

STRUGGLE FOR LIBERATION IN ZIMBABWE

The Eye of War Collaborator (Mujibha)

DHAZI CHIWAPU

www.trafford.com
North America & international
toll-free: 1 888 232 4444 (USA & Canada)
fax: 812 355 4082

TABLE OF CONTENTS

PRELUDE

This is a true narration of events experienced by the writer as far as he recalls, from the early years just as he began to follow other boys as they herd cattle in the bushes of Zimbabwe to the time Zimbabwe got independence.

The armed struggle began in 1964 and stopped on the 18th of April 1980 when Zimbabwe got independence. These events are a true reflection about what was happening across Zimbabwe then Rhodesia throughout the armed struggle.

Here is an opportunity for readers to understand the silent and unrecorded side of the struggle for independence in Zimbabwe. Independent Zimbabwe came after a harsh bloody struggle which involved every Zimbabwean in homes, bushes, refugees in the nearby countries such as Botswana, Zambia, Mozambique, Tanzania and Kenya. All these sacrificed their lives. The war was a guerrilla type, in which the fighters after being trained in foreign countries, they would cross the boarders into Zimbabwe then Rhodesia to fight the white dominated Rhodesian government under Mr Ian Douglas Smith. Mr Smith had declared unilateral declaration of independence (UDI), from the British colonial master in 1965. He went further to swear that, "Never in thousand years would Rhodesia be ruled by blacks". He ruled with oppression upon blacks, resulting in blacks to rise and seek for help to fight this oppressive regime.

The book seeks to clarify the relationship between the freedom fighters (comrades) and the people (mass) as that of fish to water. Fish in this analogue, represents the comrades and water representing the mass. In this struggle, comrades did not have to carry water, food, clothing, and medication. These were supplied by the mass. The mass also ensured safety and security for the comrades. It is with this background that the writer equates the comrades to fish and people to water. Fish will dry and die without water. Who therefore was more important in this struggle, the mass, or the comrades?

In the struggle, everyone had their unique responsibilities. The writer feels that these have not been properly recognised by the Zimbabwean's Mugabe government, so the reason for this book. The book meant to appreciate the work done by every Zimbabwean, fathers, mothers, boys (mujibhas) and girls (chimbwidos) throughout the armed struggle.

The writer, though born after the launching of the liberation struggle, was actively involved throughout the last three quarters of the struggle as a war collaborator so he has the opportunity to write about events he participated in, as far as he can remember. It is the opportunity for readers to hear everything from the horse's mouth.

There is no exaggeration in this book. What happened in the eyes of the writer might have been also happening across the country especially in the war zones such as Mt Darwin, Rushinga, Mutoko, Murehwa, Manica Land, Nyanga, Chinhoyi, Matabele Land, Chikwalakwala, Gonarezhou, and the whole of Zimbabwe at large.

It is however significant to note that as always the nature of war, it will never be exactly the same all over, so people might have been affected differently depending on region, age, and time. Some people experienced it much earlier, others very late and some not at all. However, in the Rushinga and Mt Darwin Districts, people experienced war quite earlier than other places. This was due to the geographical positions of these areas as they are situated along the border with Mozambique. It is significant to note that Chinhoyi was the first area in which exchange of fire arms took place; this was way back in 1965.

During the struggle, thousands of lives and their domestic animals perished. The Rhodesian government had to use biological means to kill domestic animals which they perceived to be of economic resources to perpetuate the struggle. Sadly, after liberation, no compensation was received by those who lost their possessions, instead, they found themselves in yet another war as Comrade Mugabe continued to seek re-election throughout his period of ruling.

The reader should know that Zimbabwe was known as Rhodesia named after a Scottish man known as Mr Cecil John Rhodes whose ambitions were to conquer Africa and build a railway line from Cape Town to Cairo.

Before that, Rhodesia was known as Zimbabwe (The Big House of Stones); this was way back before the colonial era. Between 1978 and 1979, Zimbabwe was named Zimbabwe Rhodesia under Bishop Abel Muzorewa, who ruled for less than a year during that period. However, Bishop Muzorewa did not stay longer as it soon became Zimbabwe again in 1980 on the 18th of April, under the rule of the first black Prime Minister Comrade Robert Gabriel Mugabe who is currently still the president of Zimbabwe today 2012, for thirty-two years.

Zimbabwe is also under the new Prime Minister, Mr Morgan Tsvangirai who went into coalition government after defeating the ZANU PF party for the first time in 2008 as he lead the Movement for Democratic Change Party.

The writer would like to wish Zimbabwe a bright future as it thrives to regain its status as the bread basket of Africa once again.

CHAPTER ONE

We Used to Play on Mother Zimbabwe's Face

Those days, boys and girls used to play under the dim light of the moon during the autumn nights after all the harvest had been collected from the fields and safely stored in the silos. I was just about five years as far as I can remember. In 1970, I used to follow my brother as he took the herd of cattle to the grazing forests. While out there, my brother and the other boys would collect wild fruits into their fibre bags (nhava). They would collect as much as possible and put values on each according to demand. I remember one day as I was collecting some fruits from a bushy tree on an anti-hill, I found myself flying down the hill crying all my voice out. The pain of something stinging me could not be described by anyone, it cut deep into my heart. After about a kilometre run, I stopped, only to find the other boys laughing at me. One of the big boys said to me, "Young, now you have qualified to be a herd boy, you are free to join us any time. You are a brave boy." I looked at my brother Lazarus, who smiled but I could tell he did not want me to bear the pain. He softly touched my head and said, "You are a brave boy brother, big boys never cry, isn't it?" He encouraged me to remain tough and strong, as he took a fruit from his bag and gave to me. The pain that had encompassed my body cells disappeared. I settled to enjoy my fruit. While I had just started to enjoy the fruit, the big boy dropped a bomb shell as he demanded to compare how faster I could run in a normal situation as he had already been convinced that I was very fast when I got stung by the wasps. It is now that I realised his psychological tricks to ask me to stop some of the cattle that were getting astray. He called me names such as 'Big Boy,' and 'Laston!' This made me feel stronger and stronger, eventually. "Laston! Hey Big Boy!" the bossy voice sounded. "Can you run faster than you had just done? I am keeping the clock, run and drive those cattle Biggy!" I accelerated down the slopes, jumping every bush in a show off fashion. I totally forgot about the pain, however, my eye had now got swollen.

Stings from wasps are common in the bushes in my area. There are different types of wasps, some are big and dark brown we call them marumamombe in Shona. If you get the sting from them, you will have a headache. Some are small light brown and dark brown in colour, we call them kabanda musoro. If these sting you, you experience the sharpest pain which cuts deep in your heart. The good thing is that the pain does not continue for long, but, in either case, you will get swollen. This was the type I got the sting from.

We could spend the whole day looking after cattle deep in the forests far away from home. When we became hungrier, we used to take baobab fruits, and make holes using pointed stones, and then we would start to milk those cows that had calves. I enjoyed this game most. The bad thing was that the rule of law would be to milk the cow without tying its legs, and you had to milk directly into the fruit through the tiny hole until you are satisfied about the collection. This was to me as hard as it would be to grind a pebble of stone with molars. I remember the first time I tried to do this game. I was very hungry, actually I felt hungrier when all the boys had collected their own and refused to share with me as they feasted.

After preparing my fruit, I approached one of the cows which I used to think was friendly. I made all the familiar sounds to stop it. I mentioned its name, 'Manyenye! Sviyo sviyo sviyo! Manyenye! Stop!' I constantly said this to ensure my safety. Manyenye was one of the most beautiful animals I had ever seen. It had black and white coloured skin, with horns that shaped like a buffalo's horns. I was so sure it would comply with my demands as I trusted. When it stopped, I softly crawled and tucked myself under its belly. I pulled one of the teats and struggled to squeeze the milk into my fruit. I tried harder but there was just a drop which missed the hole of the fruit and landed on my hand. When I thought I was using all my strength, I just found myself biting the dust. The cow had just kicked me away as it jumped forward. The other boys were laughing at me as I dusted myself from the ground. I just thought in my mind, that the beautiful Manyenye was just a beast which could not answer my scorn, although the laughing boys deserved it.

My brother had to share his fruit yoghurt with me.

There were lots of other funny games we played out there. Sometimes we used to play in the sands. One of the games I did not like was burying each other in the sand. In this game, we would make a trench on the river bed and asked one to lie in, and then cover the whole body under, leaving the head covered with his shirt to allow free circulation of air thereby avoiding suffocation. The other boys would disappear and hide. I experienced that it was very difficult for one to come out of the sand as it would be too heavy. One main causes of fear was the wild animals. There were lots of baboons, leopards, wild pigs, snakes and others. It was more horrific if you managed to come out and found yourself lonely. The only sound you could hear would be cicadas and birds mixed with wild cries. This was the time I would be thinking about my mother and wished I had not followed the boys.

The other game I enjoyed most was shooting grasshoppers with bows and arrows. We learnt how to make bows out of sticks and fibres and used thick grass and thorns as arrows. We would embark on a mission, to hunt the grasshoppers in the tall grass of the river banks. Every kill would be dropped in our fibre bags. The negative in this game was that the cattle would easily get astray while playing or you would find one of the old man from the nearby field beating you for letting your cattle into his field. Herding cattle was one memorable duty one would have in life.

At sun set, we would collect all our cattle and count them before we herd home. Going home was funny and enjoyable. We would begin to trot the cattle and sing songs which made our animals to speed towards the village. The dust would cover us as if a wheel wind was blowing onto us. We did not notice how the dust got into our mouths, ears and noses. My cousin Oliver's face would look like a young monkey whose teeth had not grown. His nostrils streamed with brownish mucus on which the brown dust accumulated. As he sung, I could count the number of teeth on his gums showing the gaps between them. His body skin looked as if he had been rolling where my mother had been pilling ashes for many years. There were no shoes on our feet which showed cracks on the dry and hard skin to show that bathing was only done on Christmas day. Some of Oliver's toe nails had been swiped off by sharp protruding stones on the ground. Even though the stones plucked off our nails, no one cared. Life was easy going and enjoyable.

I recall one day as we rushed home in the same manner, a stone hooked off the nail from my left big toe. I just bent down to quickly plucked it off and threw it away before covering the wound with dry sand to stop the bleeding, then limped very fast to catch up with the other boys. You speak about pain and infection? Those were out of vocabulary.

By the way, all I said about Oliver could be true about all the boys including myself, only that I could not see myself since we had no mirrors. Maybe Oliver had a far worse picture of me, it would not surprise.

Our animals knew their directions and systematically they would divide as they entered into their respective kraals before we closed them in. Thereafter, each man would part ways to their mothers' houses.

CHAPTER TWO

Playing Under the Big Moon

After supper, the elders and young would sit around the fire and began to tell tales. I did enjoy this, but sometimes I used to fear for my back especially if the tale was a horror one. I would imagine that the lion mentioned was about to snatch me from the back, so I would tuck myself under my mother's arms. Some of the tales made me to feel sorry for some of the characters. In my mind, I would have a thought of someone I knew, and assumed that he or she could be the individual, and then I would feel really sorry for such a person as if it was a reality.

One such tale was named, 'Ngwandiwe'. This was a beautiful women married at a bigamy. She was so loved by her husband and was so favoured. The old wife became very jealous and thought of fixing her. Ngwandiwe was also kind and humble. She respected her sister in-law pretty well. That time women used to grind millet using stones which were made by a specialist to fulfil their purposes. Ngwandiwe had a permanent place where she set her grinding stone. The older jealousy wife decided to dig a hole where Ngwandiwe used to kneel whenever she was grinding. The wicked woman made the hole big and covered it as a trap. The next time the beautiful Ngwandiwe knelt; she fell in and got trapped. The heartless woman rushed and closed the hole with the grinding stone. No one knew where Ngwandiwe was except Mbadza the name of the older wife which meant the cobra in vernacular. The tale goes on to say the beautiful lady spent months. Mbadza was now using the grinding stone herself, and whenever she was grinding, she would be singing a song which suggested that she was now in charge and using everything that belonged to Ngwandiwe. They said Ngwandiwe would be heard singing together with Mbadza whenever she used the grinding stone. Her voice had grown thinner and weaker. After long searching weeks passed by, the husband noticed that whenever Mbadza was using Ngwandiwe's grinding stone, she would be singing the same song, and sounded two voices would be singing. One day, he pretended to be like Mbadza and used the grinding stone while Mbadza had gone to the well to fetch some water. He also sung Mbadza's usual song. As usual, Ngwandiwe started to reply to the song. The man was alarmed to hear a voice responding from under the grinding stone. He made an alarm, the local men did not procrastinate before they congregated to help him dig out. It did not take long before they accessed and pulled out the weak and emaciated body of the once beautiful Ngwandiwe almost dying. She was fed and cared for before she started to bloom again. Mbadza was attacked with stones and got buried where she died.

This story had lots of lessons for us young ones. It discouraged us from marrying two or more wives, it also disciplined us, and taught us that lust must never be a person's characteristic. Our elders knew well that they were shaping our lives by these tales. Great philosophers they were.

Most of the times, as we played under the bright moonlight, we enjoyed going up and down the road where we would meet friends from the village across the river. We would play football made out of old rags and plastics. One of my cousins was skilful in making good balls. We would pay him with the fruits for the balls he made for us.

The other game my brother Lazarus used to lead in was role playing, as a teacher and the rest as pupils. We would do spellings, algebra, and sports. Those who excelled would be given prices in form of fruits which the boys collected during the day from the grazing forests. It was so precious and unforgettable period back then.

Years passed by, I grew to take my part in the family, already having well moulded for the roles to come. Brother Lazarus had to leave for Salisbury the great sun shine city of the then Rhodesia. To search for employment, while I took up his duties in the family. His departure caused misery and loneliness as everyone missed him greatly, not because there were no other people around, but his place had no one to match. He was always within my heart. I loved him to such an extent that I could fight anyone whom I perceived to be a threat to his life. Such happened one of those days, when I was about four years old, he was playing wrestling with other boys, and I thought they were attacking him; I just picked a long stick which I tried to stick at the buttocks of the biggest boy whose short had two big holes as if he had huge eyes on his buttocks. All the boys ran away leaving my brother free. I loved my brother.

That time, during the day, we used to run towards the road whenever the army trucks were passing by. The army people used to throw beef cans for us and we enjoyed ourselves. We used to sing songs to them and waived at them in gratification. Girls used to play nhodo, chiware and njore by day while elderly brewed and drank the seven days beer called masese, gununzvu and kachasu. They would be playing drums and mbira in jubilation. What a life on top of our motherland Zimbabwe then Rhodesia under the white leadership of Mr Ian Douglas Smith the British colonial master.

Everybody wished if such a life could be eternal. Not realising the sufferings politics had brought on our land.

CHAPTER THREE

Some Causes for War

The colonial master, the men without knees, I refer to those who came to our motherland, Africa by ship on sea, by aeroplane in the sky and on land by horses. He conquered the land and the minds of the natives. His pink skin, he described as white and the brown native man's skin, he called black. White colour symbolising peace, happiness and tranquillity, while black colour symbolising evil, sorrowfulness, unhappiness, and cursed. The native man accepted and believed as he was taught that the master was always right and never lied. He portrayed himself as the life giver for the natives as if he was ever existing time immemorial, yet, he had just intruded into a peaceful land. He found the natives developing their lives at their own pace. They lived in harmony with their environment. The land was fertile fruitful and sustained lives of various animals upon which he killed for food. He collected fruits for food. At his pace, he manufactured his own tools and shaped his life and environment. He owned his land and looked after it the way God had created. He enjoyed life in his sovereignty right.

Happiness and ownership of his land ceased not long after the colonial master landed. All fertile land was confiscated. The natives were pushed out to the rocky infertile land. The master established himself and established institutions. Schools, hospitals, cities, roads, motor cars, buses, bicycles and aeroplanes, characterised the new life which according to the master was a modern life. The master, introduced 'a modern life' as if the natives had no modern life of their own. The master refused to recognise the native man's life as modern. His was special and nothing better.

Seeing all these, the natives totally believed that the master was indomitable and was directly communicating with God and all his questions answered right. The native had no choice but to answer, 'Yes Bass! Yes Ngosi! Yes Nkosi! Yes Master!" The native was taught the overseas stories, which revealed more about his ingenuity and superiority. He was not a human being in his eyes. He did not have problems in his life. It was a taboo to see a white man begging for food in the streets. It would turn the world upside down to see the white man ill. Not realising that the colonial government had full responsibilities upon the welfare of its people. He was rich and powerful, no one could stand against such a super human being. The man from the land across the deep waters, the land he referred to as the developed countries, in which everything seemed green like the Garden of Eden. This is the land all natives thought it was like heaven. Everyone wished to be on this land.

The belief that Britain particularly England and the United States of America are lands of all possibilities is embedded in most people who have never been in these countries even today. Just going to England appeared to transform someone's life. Most people believed that oversea trained doctors, teachers, lawyers, nurses are far too superior over those trained in Africa. They had no idea about the unspeakable problems in those lands. It is only when one lands overseas and suffered the calamities of the real life in the dream lands that their eyes open. One will realise how blessed they are wherever they are in the 'undeveloped' or the so called third world.

Parents encouraged their children to excel in their studies so as to increase the opportunities of going overseas. Their dreams, only if all their children could cross the deep waters and make it to the other side, life would become the Garden of Eden.

Really? Is it ever green in America? Is it really ever flowing honey in Britain? German? France? Russia? Or China? The master had without doubt dominated the brain cells of the natives. There was or is no one to convince them that life is not the way portrayed. Those natives who managed to cross the seas in those days made it worse. They returned having changed physically, psychologically and politically. Their skins changed lighter in brown even though they were darker before they left. They spoke differently and seemed to be more educated. They put on suits and looked smarter than they were before. They managed to buy more and owned things they could not afford before. They presented as though they dropped from heaven. They did not like to reveal the true way of life across the seas. Not realising that some worked as Health Care Assistants. Jobs in which young people as they are care for adults. In such a job, young people show their kind hearts, their desire to see continuity of life even-though the adult is dead. Empathy, warmth, and love to see someone living being the major characteristics one must have. The young people see the unforeseen as they execute the job diligently. However, their tender backbones would be the target. As a result, some suffer from back pains while young as such, which eventually send their lives bed bound.

Eying all these, how could anyone who has never been in those lands believe there were probably more problems for anyone in the diaspora? If one tried to tell the truth about the hardships overseas, they would be accused of being a blocker to prosperity. People would think such would be selfish, only to keep themselves the cream of the society. On the other hand, if one attempted to encourage hard working and dedication as the source of success, he would be labelled as a traitor, a colonised person. In political set up, you would be equal to the colonial master. Not realising that prosperity is end product of hard working and dedication. Nothing comes out of nothing. To get something out of it, you have to put something into it. That is what I call, the law of survival.

The master had dug deeper, and spread his tentacles everywhere. He was like the owner of the land. He settled and owned fertile lands whose sizes they pegged using horses. My great grandfather Chief Changamire Makuni told me long ago, that, to mark the length of a farm, a horse would have to die running that would be the position of the first peg. Four horses would die running in order to completely peg one farm. Everything encircled in that farm including the people and their domestic animals would belong to the master. That time ago, there were no news reporters. The world could not even realise the fate of anyone resisting the forced labour. Some, were shot dead, others were buried alive to intimidate and silence the living. In Rhodesia, there were many such periods as chibharo (forced labour), and nguva yemakandiwa (the period of the storm drains). These were the periods during which the master was using the natives as forced labourers to develop farms and other infrastructures. Many lives were lost unreported. The natives were treated in horrific manners. The worst method of torturing was known as mbarambatotya, this was a flat plank about fifty centimetres long, on one end had six inch nails to make spikes. That would be the side the master used to punch the buttocks or the hands of the natives who resisted them. After several punches on the palms, with blood splashing in all directions, he would be forced to hold the handle of a hoe, axe or pick to dig or cut logs of hard wood.

Who answered the cries of them all as they wailed in those forests? Only God knows. The second weapon which remained in use till the end of the apartheid era was the dog. As he dug the ground, as he continuously cut trees, from dawn to dusk he must not have stretched his back. He must not have talked nor looked at his country man who was wailing and dying for help on his right or left side. Who might have been dragged dead and dumped into the woods? As soon as he did that, a dog mulled flesh from the left buttock. If he did that again, flesh would be from the right side buttock. Some would die digging, from the loss of blood, they would be the food for hyenas, a lesson to others.

No man today, can explain the suffering endured by those people for one to understand.

Such actions, lead to the first war against the master, The First Chimurenga War, in which a courageous woman named Nehanda was the leader. The natives were crushed to dust in that war, as the master used his advanced weapons. Those who tried to fight, used stones, sticks, spears and shields. Bullets penetrated the shields to destroy their bare chests condemning them to death. They courageously fought, to defend their land, they died and no decent burial held for them all. That was the war in which the courageous young lady whose name was Nehanda was killed by hanging. But before she died she had warned the master that her bones would rise. Indeed, the bones arose in the second Chimurenga War which is the centre of this book.

The cruelty and the suffering of the natives escalated after and during these wars.

Critically speaking, the idea of developing this country was not bad at all. Today, people are proud of their country due to its beautiful cities, good network of roads, schools hospitals and water supply resources. Credits to those who perished. It is however, the dehumanising manner in which natives were not treated as people. The master did not realise that in any way, if a foreigner intruded into your land and started to behave and act as the owner, you could resist and fight too.

Yes, the native person developed into a different state, in which he confronted death instead of fear due to the suffering he endured. He arose and sought help from those countries which sympathised. The war of liberation was rekindled and named The Second Chimurenga War which was fought until the year 1980.

CHAPTER FOUR

Comrade Vhuu Commandeered the First Group into my Area

Such happiness did not last long. In 1971, the summer season was about to end, that day the sun had just gone back into its womb, darkness was creeping. I could still see the surroundings, but could not differentiate a standing person from a stump. I was hurrying my cattle down the slopes towards the village. The animals started to jump and to run faster and faster as I was becoming afraid. It was when one of our troublesome ox tried to go its own way and I was driving it to join the others when I saw something unusual. I looked at it and asked myself what this was and when did it grow there? Remember, this was my usual path all my life, so I knew everything the same way I knew the back of my hand. This thing which looked like a dried stump had never been there, yet I could not make sense out of it. I just posed for seconds, but before I ignored it, a voice came out of it, "Munin'ina usatya zvako!" (Young brother, don't be afraid). Ndiri mukoma wako, enda unoudza vakuru kuti vaungane pasi pemuuyu uyo wepamhiri perwizi nekukrumidza." (I am your brother, go and tell the elders to congregate under the baobab tree across the river)". I almost soaked myself in urine due to fear. The person was just like a standing dark stump in the middle of bushes. In Zimbabwe, there are lots of dry, burnt, turned black stumps due to years of exposure to veldt fires. This was how the standing structure from which a humble voice came. The head was covered with leaves, as if a small bushy plant had been growing above it. I could not identify the shoulders but on his back from top to bottom, I saw something which I thought was a knob carry. I had not seen anything like that since my birth. It was unbelievable that such a sweet, friendly, caring and humble voice could come from such an ugly structure. At least the voice helped to keep me alive.

At school, we had been shown a film about terrorists (magandanga) being killed so easily and eaten by hyenas. We were also told that they carried walking sticks and that we must report to the army if we came across them. A lot went on through my mind. My heart pounded like thunder storm. I did not utter a word as I continued to follow my cattle. I cannot recall how I closed the kraal. Within the shortest time I had joined other people from the village who had started streaming towards the baobab tree as directed. I was surprised to find that all the elders and young had already been well informed and cooperated. The headman, my father, my mother, my sisters and brothers had already gathered under the big tree in the thicket.

A group of about ten terrorists surrounded us as we sat in the grass. This was the first time we saw the terrorists as they were known by the Rhodesian army throughout the liberation struggle. The leader started to address us. His name was Vhuu! He was a gifted man in everything he did. His voice was not as I was thinking and heard about terrorists (magandanga). He had a sweet voice and a lovely tone such that you would urge him to continue talking. He spoke with a tone close to the Manyika language.

The man introduced his group by first saying they were the so called the terrorists (magandanga) by the Smith government. He introduced his colleagues one by one, by their names. I can still remember, Gwazai, Masango, Murotero, Tawona, Digden, Ngwena, Chabadukanyereyemhuka, Paradzai, and Mabhunumuchapera.

Vhuu told us that they were not bad people as portrayed by the Rhodesian army under Mr Ian Smith. He told us that they were our brothers who left and went to Zambia to train and returned to fight the whites. He narrated how Zimbabwe was snatched from our forefathers. That after taken, it was given a new name Rhodesia. He said they took it through Lobengula whom they tricked by giving him a mirror and a small boat and asked him to put an X as a signature on the Royal Charter from the British Queen. He told us how they fought and killed Mbuya Nehanda the spirit medium which lead them in the bush and said, before she died she had declared that her bones would arise and fight them till they returned back to Britain. He said Nehanda was the spirit medium which lead the Shona as they fought the whites in Zimbabwe based in the Mazowe Valley. He then said the group of terrorists he was leading were some of the bones Nehanda referred to. He turned and pointed at us, and said, "You brothers and sisters shall take our places in this war". He warned us that the war was going to be a long and dangerous, but it would be won. He referred to his group as comrades. Vhuu said comrades were well trained by means of magic cooking so that no bullet could kill them. He said bullets could not penetrate their flesh after proper cooking. He showed us the guns they had and how accurate and dangerous they were to kill and destroy the Rhodesian soldiers, their trucks and aeroplanes. He said nothing could stand against these weapons, they displayed sub-machine guns, motors, bazooka, machine guns, shot guns, and grenades. We were convinced that nothing could the Rhodesian army do to such equipped group of comrades.

They grouped and started to sing war songs in which we were asked to join in. The songs were so touching and motivating such that although I was very young I felt blood running up and down my body. I felt I must join, get cooked and fight for my country. The words of the songs had deep meaning and explained a lot about our country and the war to come. In the songs, I could see the new Zimbabwe and its wealth. What a moment? The whole forest was full of life and enjoyment. Young teenage boys were given the guns to hold and made as if they were at war. Vhuu referred to them as the inherent soldiers. No one liked to stop. After all, Vhuu thanked everyone, but before he dismissed us, he warned all of us that whosoever was going to report to the Rhodesian army would be known by the spirits and would be killed by them. We parted to our respective houses as we sang the songs in our hearts. Older boys were found to be singing and talking about going to Zambia to be cooked as they were eager to return and fight for their country.

CHAPTER FIVE

The First Recruits

It did not take long before the big boys from my village began to disappear one after another. I did not know they were being taken to Zambia to join the liberation struggle. No one attempted to investigate as to where they were, which sometimes set a wave of fear in me. We learnt later that my brother had also attempted to go too, but as they crossed one of the rivers, he felt as if he was carrying a heavy bag of sand on his back. He told the others that he was returning as it would imply that he would die if he had gone, so he did not go. I did not know whether this was chickening out, but I was happy with his decision because I would be with my brother as we fought the war from home, all the same. Several boys left, including my nephews, Michael Madzinga who became to be known as comrade Mhembwe, his brother Shande Charles Munhuwa who became to be Chigwazamasoramhuriyesango, my cousin Charles Chiweshe, my uncle Manius Chedare whose chimurenga name was Gylord Zimunya, my nephew Joshua Mbaza who was popularly known as Rezainocheka Bhunu and many other boys and beautiful girls, joined the ranks.

In 1971, one autumn bright sunny day, it was scotching, temperatures could have been above 30 degrees Celsius, and one could see the radiation and mirage of the heat across the golden grass far down the valley. The grass had dried turning our green forests golden. Trees were motionless. This is one of October's characteristics in my area. The forest would be live with the sounds of cicadas. There was a sign of tranquillity above the shiny backs of our cattle as they rested peacefully under the shadow of the baobab tree. One of the bulls was the only animal standing in the southern edge of the cool shade provided by the great huge baobab tree. That afternoon, my brother and other boys had decided to start milking when suddenly, "Pwaaaaa! Kaaatyaaa! waaaaaa! kakakakaka! trrrrr!"

What I heard that afternoon my ears had not heard. The sound went sharp across my head and all of us fell to the ground. No one knew what had happened. The good thing was only that this sounded once. Our cattle arose and started running in all directions as if a lion had struck in their midst.

Rats could be seen speeding from one hut to another, while dogs got their tails in between their legs and moving closer to their owners. My grandmother was brave enough to walk towards us with her hands on her back as if someone had died. Her face showed worry and many unanswered questions. Her behaviour set me to be very afraid since I trusted that she was the pillar of our safety in the village. I believed that she could stop anything that intended to harm us spiritually. This day, I believed she was not able and I thought there must have been someone whose powers were greater than hers. Her forehead showed wrinkles above her eye brows. This was the first time I saw my grandmother having such facial expressions on her face. She walked to the kraal, and stood at the entrance and whispered something which I failed to understand. I just thought she was talking to the one greater than her. Her lips were moving as she appeared to be talking to herself. She turned to the right side of the kraal, then to the left and finally she made a U-turn back to the huts without saying a word to us.

My brother tried to break the silence by a silly cough. I thought he had observed how afraid I was. I was shivering like a reed in the slow flowing water of the great Mazowe River. My skin had grown some goose pimples despite the fact that it was one of the hottest days. The jug of milk I was holding had slipped from my hands and all its contents emptied on the dry soil which showed no gratification as it sucked all and quickly dried out. I did not know what to do. My second thoughts brought the vision of my mother who was still in the fields. I wished she was with us so that I could die in her hands from this strange thing. No one could describe the source of such a sound. The only closest source was thunder, but this was autumn and the sky had no cloud to produce such a sound, more so the sound did not appear to have come from heaven. I was certain that it came from the ground but I could not tell the direction. The whole village was as silent as a grave.

After about one hour of turmoil and pandemonium my brother pointed down the road to the direction of Hokoyo Dam. He did not speak, but used head and eye signs. We all looked as he intended. From a distance, was a man who seemed to be running but struggling? He was a young man of middle age who arrived, almost breathless. We knew this man, but what we wanted was to know the news he was carrying. We surrounded him, each one of us having questions, but we could not ask. He forced his words out to say one of the men on the other side of the dam had died. He had been shot dead by the comrades accused of spying for the Rhodesian army who camped at Mary Mount Mission about twelve kilometres from our village. The man of a huge family decided to run to the camp and reported the comrades who had held the rally (pungwe) last night. His daughter was the one who secretly reported him to the comrades, who in turn, wasted no time in shooting him to set as a warning to the whole village.

The man described that the comrades arrived at Mr Mheni's compound and ordered him to call his wife. When the wife arrived, he was told to spread a mat on the ground and asked to have sexual intercourse with his wife as a farewell as he would be seeing the sun for the last time. The man did as instructed but no one could explain the last events as everybody had fallen to the ground due to the sound of the gun which cracked some people's ear drums.

After the shot, all those around could not tell where and how the comrades disappeared. Many people said they melted away. No one could identify their foot prints even as they crossed the dry clear land. From that moment, everybody believed that comrades had supernatural powers to hide in the air. Comrade Vhuu had warned the villagers about the quensequences of conniving with the enemy of the liberation. A lesson had just been given and it was loud and clear, these guys meant serious business no doubt. These were thoughts in my mind and everyone's mind I guessed. This incident transformed everything in my area. We felt that there was another killer besides the well-known witches of the village and malaria. Personally, I got to fear the new killer more than any other.

CHAPTER SIX

The Big Snake

Snakes are found all over in my area, some poisonous, others not, some such as big as pythons others tiny. It is possible to bump into any one as one walks either in the grass or on the road. I had not seen a big snake since birth, but small ones yes and I feared them so much. Those early years, I would not fear a leopard than a snake. We were told tales about different snakes, but the python I feared most because we were told it had the capacity to swallow a big man or a medium calf alive. I feared to be swallowed alive.

The elders of the village had their own means of strengthening the young people's hearts, to make them courageous and fearless. Sometimes they held initiation ceremonies in which big boys would go through some training.

One afternoon in the year 1970, the headman was in his field. Some of the fields in my area are very far from the village. The headman's field was beyond the rocky hills. In these hills were thick forests in which you would find leopards, pythons and other edible animals like rock rabbits, bucks, hares and so on. People used to hunt and make kills in these rocky hills.

The headman was busy working the soil to prepare for the rains, suddenly, he heard a buck cry. He gathered his dogs and disappeared into the grass. To his amazement, he saw the huge python swallowing a buck from the head. The monster was unfortunate that it could not run away since the huge buck's head had gone as far as its neck. The man was bold enough to chop the snack's head into two lengthwise with his axe. He pulled the buck out of its mouth and killed it as well, since it was still alive. The man had to give thanks to his ancestors behind a small bush he took some leaves and put them on the ground before he started to call the names of his ancestors as he clapped his hands in thanks given. He then had to skin the snake and hide the flesh into the huge holes and covered it such that no one could be affected by the dry skeleton. It was the skin he brought to the village for the ceremony that led me to talk about this snake. The whole village was summoned. I was one of them. As one of the children who really feared pythons, I felt a chill cutting all over my body. The man had nailed the skin to the ground in such a way that made us to think the snake was alive. It was a long python maybe four or six meters and as wide as half a meter. To me this thing was real. I then decided to attach myself to my mother; I always thought my mother could kill a lion with one blow.

Line by line, old people led as, they walked along the back of this dangerous rape tail. Courageous children followed. My mother encouraged me by asking me to put my finger on its tail. She then put me down to step on its back. I eventually walked to and from the head and tail and soon the fear had gone. I began to run to and from enjoying it every step I made. That was the beginning of my fearless behaviour which I have up to now. At that age, I began to go to the fields by myself. Our field was behind the big mountain and dangerous animals were found in them too, but I braved through. I did not bother thinking about the leopards or rumours of lions wandering about. Our great fathers were great philosophers the world had ever seen. They had all knowledge about how to prepare us for events to come. Boys and girls grew up to be the most courageous, brave and strong hearted. This is the foundation that made some boys fearlessly stood in front of the roaring guns.

CHAPTER SEVEN

The First Ambush

From the first rally on which comrade Vhuu and his group first introduced themselves to our village, in that year 1971, our life styles took a new dimension. Young boys and girls were no longer going out to play under the big white moon at night. Parents were now afraid for their children so they started to introduce their own curfews to ensure everybody was at home while the sun shined. Rallies (pungwe) with the comrades formed part of our lives' entertainment. At day time, we would gather in the so called bases (places in the bush, specifically chosen by comrades for their security.)

The death of the first man by being shot sent a clear message to all of the people in the village such that they enhanced the safety for the comrades wherever possible.

Comrade Vhuu educated the mass about how to respond and act safely in case there was a gun battle. We were taught never to run

27

upright but to bend as close to the ground as possible and to lay flat to the ground wherever possible. He taught us how to move very fast on our stomachs like snakes do. They also taught us what to do when suddenly in confrontation with the enemy. In this case people were encouraged to move away from cover and clearly raise their hands as a sign of surrendering. Many survival tactics even the way to communicate and how to keep confidential information without offending the enemy were successfully imparted to everyone. The easiness with which all people appeared to grasp these skills lead me to ponder how skilful comrade Vhuu and his group was.

Everyone was totally convinced that Mbuya Nehanda the spirit medium was leading the way. Death was no more in our vocabulary. The enemy had to be defeated, was our priority target.

Food was prepared by every mother of the village, but taken to the bases by the young girls (chimbwidos) under the escort of the young boys (mujibhas). The comrades formulated structures and educated the people about their responsibilities. Mujibhas were the spying agents and informers as well as vehicles to carry armoury from place to place and to shop for the comrades. Chimbwidos were to spent time with the comrades carrying food, water and washing for them. They could cook food when the parents were in the fields. Parents had extensive responsibilities to ensure constant supply of utilities and to link groups of comrades from faraway places.

Surprisingly, the comrades told the people (mass) that they were not supposed to eat any other food except meat and sadza. Derere and Round nuts were completely out of the menu because they stated that, whoever ate them would surly become weak and bullet target in event of crossfire.

One night in summer, the bush had grown good foliage for cover and it had just rained. We were all called for a rally situated close to the top of the cliff. We had quite a marvellous time singing and dancing, learning and praying to the spirit mediums that were represented by the famous Mbuya Nehanda. We were taught that Nehanda was the spirit medium who would ensure no one died in this war. Slogans such as, 'Pamberi neChimurenga! Chimurenga chekusunungura Zimbabwe! Zanu! Iwe neni tine basa! Basa! Rekusunungura Zimbabwe! (Forward with the war of Chimurenga! Chimurenga! To liberate Zimbabwe! Zanu! You and I have the duty! The Duty! To liberate Zimbabwe!)'. Such slogans set our adrenaline high, such that our minds had nothing else but to fight to liberate our country at all cost. In our minds, there was nothing good any enemy would do so he had to be removed.

We were taught about the ZANU's leadership structure. Comrade Ndabaningi Sithole was the president of the party stationed in Zambia. Comrade Herbert Chitepo was the Chairman and comrade Takawira had just died. Comrades Nkomo, Mugabe, Tekere, Tongogara and many others were in prison.

This particular night was rich with information. People were enjoying everything when suddenly comrade Vhuu stood and talked as if he was possessed. He said he was seeing the enemy soldiers still very far but they were able to see everything taking place in the night. He immediately dismissed us according to the directions of our houses. Each group was led by a comrade to ensure their safety back home. So we swiftly and safely parted. My brother and I were still singing and reflecting on what our dear comrades had said, before one by one we were taken into dreams.

The following morning, as we went to the fields with my mother and sisters, we observed that the comrades had crossed over to the mountains westwards further from our village. We saw the foot prints as they crossed the fields in the night.

The day continued as normal. We were busy hoeing the field when maybe because my back felt numb, I stretched it as I cast my eyes in the sky, up in the sky, appeared two very big birds as big as a hen, they were black with white edged wings. They were flying against each other so fiercely such that a hissing sound could be heard from behind the mountains. When they collided, a thunderous sound could be heard. My mother said to us, these birds implied that something dangerous would follow. She told us to leave the field and warned that we should not return home but to go to her sister's place behind the other mountain. However, before we left the field, four helicopters we heard flying towards that mountain where we suspected the comrades to have gone. Within a flush of light, two fighter jets flew in from nowhere dropping thunderous bombs and left swiftly living thunderous smoky and confusing atmosphere. There were different sounds of thunder I heard that day. I could not explain or describe what passed through my ears during that time. My head was as if sounds were from all directions. This was the first of such encounter in my life. The worst part was that my mother had decided to take us to her sister's place not aware that this war was closer to the sister's place than our home and the way was mountainous, bushy and ferocious.

We trotted with our hands above our heads afraid that we could get bombed by mistake. We bolted our way through to the village under the trees and got to my auntie's houses. The journey which took us just over an hour. We found them in the shadow of death.

They told us that three people had died. These were one father who died carrying his child as they ran away. The other was a boy of fifteen a mujibha who was with the comrades in the base. We could smell the gun powder smoke bellowing from the nearby mountain. Life seemed to have been sucked out of the world. Not even a bird whispered. I remained tucked to my mother.

We spent the night at my auntie's place and returned home the following morning.

When we got home, we were told exactly what had happened in the battlefield during yesterday's encounter. The chimbwidos who were with the comrades narrated the story. The girls told us that things were as calm and music was playing loud and sweet. During the war, rumba music from Kenya, Zaire (Congo), and Tanzania was popular. It formed part of the entertainment to keep our minds happy and enjoying to forget about the realities of war. The girls said tea and lunch had just been served and people were sitting in poshtos (subdivisions of the base where comrades sat in smaller groups). They said one of the girls decided to go a bit further in the grass to relieve herself. After that, she started to pull some of the grass she wanted to plait while relaxing in the poshto. Unfortunately, that girl was under surveillance from the Rhodesian army who had closed in ready to attack. When the girl was walking back, a gunfire started, followed by the bombs from the jets. The war grew to what I already discussed above. However, after the gun firings had ceased, comrade Vhuu was reported to have gone round from poshto to poshto picking the guns left by the other comrades who had fled without their guns. As comrade Vhuu went round, he found that girl fainted flat in the grass. Comrade Vhuu tried to wake her up in vain. He took a blanket and put the girl on his back. He continued to pick the guns and placed some on the right shoulder and others on the left shoulder. Before he left, he made some shots towards the direction he perceived the enemy to be. What a courageous fighter? Comrade Vhuu went down the river where he saw one of the comrades trapped between two roots of a tree that had been exposed by the flowing water. My dear comrade had tried to put his head in the event of trying to hide from the bullets during the battle, but could not remove his head. Vhuu helped his comrade and he got a hand to carry some of the guns.

Comrades had a plan set before they got to a place. They would plan how and where to meet if under sudden attack. Comrade Vhuu met his colleagues at their place of meeting very far from the battle field. Some of his comrades he punished by confiscating their guns for few days. Comrades were never supposed to part with their guns by any means. They would be disciplined for doing so. How could a soldier part ways with his weapon for it was the means to make him or her a soldier? His or her life was in the barrel of the gun.

By the way all this time that fainted girl was still on comrade Vhuu's back. Comrade Vhuu tried to ask the girl to come down, but she clung tight at his back. Comrade Vhuu decided to take her to a faraway village in the Pfungwe area across the Mazowe River, there our dear girl came to her senses and agreed to climb down. The great comrade Vhuu handed her to the villagers and directed them to escort the girl back to her place in chief Makuni's Diwa area. The girl was safely returned to her place. She also played a big role in telling this story.

This encounter marked the onset of fully blown war in Chief Makuni's area within the Rushinga district to the North Eastern side of Zimbabwe. This is the area on which this book is centred. Chief Makuni's area is a vast land which stretches into Mozambique to the eastern side forming The Hira Border Post. To the western side the Murowa River runs from the Jirichiri mountains down all the way to the great Mazowe River to the Southern for about forty kilometres. Murowa River forms the boundary between the Makuni area and the Rusambo area on its upper part half way. On the southern part, it forms a boundary with the Kamanika's area which leads into The Mazowe River. The Mazowe River meanders north eastern towards the mighty Zambezi River forming a boundary between Makuni and Murehwa on the upper part and the remainder with Uzumba Maramba Pfungwe. To the eastern, is the last village known as Chiyero which forms a boundary with the Chitange area. The border continues into the Hira Border Post where Zimbabwe and Mozambique meet. The border stretches up the Ruya River rounding the Nyagwiti, Nyabanda up the Nyamakate River, forming a boundary with the Masososo areas in Chief Rusambo's area back to the Jirichiri Mountains all the way forming a boundary with Chief Rusambo's area before joining the Murowa River again. It forms an area of about 3600km2.

This area played a great role in the liberation of Zimbabwe since it was the entry point to and from Mozambique. It's borders with Mozambique were populated with land mines planted by the Rhodesian government to kill the comrades and whoever attempted to cross the borders. Many civilians, comrades as well as Rhodesian soldiers lost their lives in the forests of this area. Today, these borders are still claiming lives of children and animals as some of the land minds are still to be cleared.

The ZANLA FORCES under Comrade Josiah Magama Tongogara as the chief commander and comrade Rex Nhongo (Mujuru) his deputy, were the key operators in this area. So most of the activities in this book involved the ZANLA Forces rather than the ZIPRA Forces who operated from Zambia to the western parts of Zimbabwe.

CHAPTER EIGHT

Shock at our Primary School

Our primary school is called Nyamanyanya School, named after the Nyamanyanya Mountains in which the first encounter took place. The school is situated about 300 meters from the main road, and about five kilometres from the mountains. To the eastern side is a small river on which Hokoyo Dam is situated. This is where people and animals used to drink from during the war. The bridge was just less than a kilometre from the school.

That day, there was peace at our school; lessons were as good as ever. We were having a radio lesson that morning. The radio teacher was Mrs Childs who I did think originated from Britain, to teach us skills in English. I enjoyed this lesson so much because I liked talking in English although I did not understand much. When Mrs Childs greeted us, we would all answer with one voice such as, "Good morning Mrs Childs!" when Mrs Childs said, "Well done children!"

I would feel very happy thinking that she heard my voice. While in the middle of such a beautiful lesson, the devil overshadowed our school. "Crack! Crack! Guuuu! Tatatsrarararerrrrrrrr!

Pwaaaaaa! Tiguuuu! Tiguuu! Went the cracking and thunderous sounds. Impulsively all of us including the teacher found ourselves flat on the floor. Straying bullets we heard hissing and breaking the windows. I smelt death. You ask me how it smells. No one can describe it for you to understand unless you smell it yourself. Up to now, I have never smelt anything like that, which is the only reason why I think it was death. The guns continued to thunder and cracking for a while before silence followed. It was a dead silence, no bird nor was insect heard. The whole school with its over six hundred pupils was dead silent. The headmaster Mr Mavhunga, was a courageous man. He was the only one we saw walking from class to class telling the teachers to keep all the children in their respective classes for safety reasons.

It did not take long before four helicopters started hovering above us. The helicopters made a deafening noise. At one time I thought it had landed on the roof of our classroom. Suddenly, two of them landed on our playground. The Rhodesian soldiers jumped out one by one and ran in a single file to our classes. They spread and simultaneously instructed all the pupils to assembly. This we did within a flush of light. One huge bearded soldier spoke with a hoarse voice, saying they were aware of all the boys who had gone to join the terrorists in Zambia from the villages. He also said he was going to flush out the relatives of all those boys and they would be punished if they told lies. They started with my nephew Takawira whose brother Joshua the one who was popularly known as Rezainocheka Bhunu who operated in the Manikaland region.

The young boy was in grade two barely eight years old. He was held by the right side ear and dragged like a pig to the slaughter. The boy screamed with a troubled voice. He could not even call his mother in the cry, but it was a cry of a child who was so afraid and was seeing death in his eyes. They pulled him aside where they slapped him with a crackling slap on the right side chick. The cry intensified. All the children were shaking and shivering like reeds in flowing water. Some had their pants soaked in urine. One of the Grade One girls was found defecating and rolling on the ground with fear.

Takawira was taken from us, we saw him leading them to his home which was not far from the bridge on which the ambush had taken place. I watched them all those massive huge men, heavily armed following the poor boy until one by one, as they disappeared behind the rocks towards the bridge. My mind and soul was troubled as I had flashes of imagining what was going to happen to Takawira. I had thoughts about what if it was me. Takawira had just been swallowed by the rocks which were eventually swallowed by the thick forest.

One of the young teachers in his thirties, was just unfortunate, he was targeted, picked and they started to punch him. Two of the soldiers we saw exchanging to kick the helpless teacher as though they were playing football. His head was swollen and bleeding through the nose. It was horrific. The children could not take it anymore. They looked miserable and wanting. No one to cuddle them, no not even their loved parents could not comfort them. We thought our teachers were strong to protect us, but, we realised that they were vulnerable too.

The soldiers left our school in shock and disbelief, but Takawira was gone. He was my closest friend, the child of my auntie. A lot went through my head, was he killed? This I was convinced was the truth. I had deep shock and fear for his life as they disappeared into the thicket. The big soldier ordered us to run home. The whole school was filled with children as they scattered in all directions to their respective homes. I went straight home to my mother.

Later that evening, came the news I was looking the answer for. Takawira was safe home with his mother. What had happened was that one of the chimbwidos had reported to the soldiers about the disappearance of Takawira's brother who had gone to Zambia. She had told them to ask the young brother Takawira to confirm. Throughout the Chimurenga War, incidents like these happened regularly. Many people lost their lives after someone wrongly reported either to the comrades or to the Rhodesian Army through hatred or fear. There was no justice.

CHAPTER NINE

Our Parents Snatched From Us

Whenever there is war, there are causalities. The events that took place in my area so far included the arrival of the comrades, the death of one man shot by the comrades. The encounter that took place in the Nyamanyanya Mountains as well as the ambush that shook our school. These left the face of our society totally volatile and transformed. There was a mixture of sadness and happiness. Sadness in that a lot of negatives were characterising our way of life, happiness in that we were promised a free Zimbabwe if the war ended. Our friendly forests were alive with a new breed of animals in human form. The Rhodesian army were found all over in mountains, plains and homes hunting for the terrorists. On the other hand, the comrades were all over and multiplying fast. Our area was like a boiling pot, we expected anything at any time. Boys and girls disappeared, and then followed by families disappearing into Mozambique. There was nowhere people could run to hide.

What disturbed me as a young boy was the act of missing the loved ones. We could not tell what happened or where some of them had gone. No shoulder to cry on. It was just like the Shona proverb which says, the mother got burnt on her back and the child got burnt on its stomach, so how could the mother carry a baby on her back without problems? The Smith regime unleashed a wave of violence against the people. Accusing them of keeping, helping and feeding the terrorists. Initially, every person above the age of nine years was regarded as a potential terrorist. I recall one morning, I woke up to find the whole village under serge. There were Rhodesian soldiers everywhere. Young children could be seen confused walking aimlessly. Many seemed to have questions as to what to do but no one could speak. Some of the soldiers were so cruel. There was a short red faced soldier whom I saw breaking the doors of our huts with the buttock of his gun. My mother came out under shock. She tried to close the door, alas, she was knocked so hard right on the left shoulder which gave her a problem till her death. I started to cry helplessly when I saw my mother under such brutality. No one could listen. The worst was that, most of them spoke in English and yet most of the villagers could not clearly understand. There were two black soldiers who spoke in Karanga. We saw that they used their fingers to form a V shape, so they would ask if you understood the sign. All those who understood were not troubled. I did not understand this up to this day what V represented.

They forced-march all the people and ordered them to sit under the big baobab tree. The army stood around us. I happened to sit in the centre in attempt to hide from these cruel soldiers. As we sat like sheep ready to be slaughtered, we heard a cracking sound from the back of the house behind us. One of the leaders counted six big men to go behind the house. They were surprised to see one of the fathers lying dead in the pool of blood which gushed out of his head. He had been shot dead by that notorious short cruel soldier. The man was taken away from us just like that. My brain was like boiling water, as I could not describe the feelings. At one point I thought about the man who had been killed by the comrades now this one, I found myself encircled by killers, nowhere to report. I felt helpless and at that age gave my life to anything that could happen. Death became nothing to be feared. The soldiers asked questions in English, I just heard voices, but could not make meaning out of them. The two black soldiers helped with translation. Most of the questions were seeking to know where the terrorists were. They educated the people about how to treat the terrorists to make them suffer and to report them as soon as possible. They taught people that terrorists would all easily be killed by the use of their helicopters, bombardiers, army trucks and their advanced guns. They told us these terrorists had lice, smelt, ate wild fruits and would cause suffering among the people so they were not to be supported by any means. They also distributed pamphlets about comrade Vhuu who they said if anyone helped them to catch him, they would get $10.000.00 as a price.

After about four hours of torture and starvation, all our fathers were ordered to jump into the army trucks. My father was one of these men. When the soldiers and our fathers left, that was the last time we saw some of them, others were seen ten years later after the end of the war in 1980. My father spent two years in the unknown land. He said he was in Wawa prison. He told us lots of stories about hardships encountered by war prisoners. He said some committed suicide as a result. It was so sad to learn about such mistreatment to the human body. On the other hand, I was excited to be with my father again. Many children grew without their fathers and up to now some do not have any ideas what happened to their fathers. It left for young children to fend for themselves and younger siblings. I recall how life became unbearable when my father was in prison. Gradually, I was starting to believe that my brother who was nearly fifteen years old was my father. This led me to go and look for a job as a herd boy at the local shop. In this job, I encountered all abuses one might think about. I used to work with a ten year old boy. Looking after over fifty cattle was not an easy duty. We used to leave home before breakfast with our cattle and spent the day in the forest, hungry and thirsty only to return home in the dark. One day we lost two calves. We did not return home on time. The night was so dark that I started to fear for my life. As we negotiated our way home, hungry and tired as we were, hyenas started laughing behind us sending a chilling fear within us. I turned to check if my back was safe, by the time I looked forward, my colleague had disappeared. This was the night in which I ran faster than any form of hurricane. It did not take moments before we got home. My colleague was already in the kitchen eating food. I had no idea how he got in, since we did not have the keys. When I called him to open the door, he refused arguing that I could have done what he did. I had no idea how he got in. Fear and hunger haunted me. He started to mock at me as he helped himself with the best meat which had been prepared for the owner of the shops. There was no chance for me so I went to sleep as hungry as I was. This was how difficulty life was. The following morning, the owner of the shop summoned me to enquire about who had eaten the chicken meat last night. I was afraid to say, because I knew that I would be beaten everyday out there by my colleague if he knew I reported him. I think the shop owner cleared me, maybe he saw my innocence.

The job was as difficulty, but we were paid 40 cents every month. I remember my first forty cents salary, I gave it to one of the old man who had come to buy from the Chidavaenzi Store to go and give my mother so as for her to buy mealy meal to feed my sisters. The man did give my mother, but, my mother told me that she was robbed of the money when she had gone to the big shops at Mary Mount Mission. I was troubled more and more thinking maybe the man robbed her. After working for two more months, I woke up one very early morning before dawn and decided to run to my home as a way to free myself. The war had shaped young children to become responsible adults as a survival mechanism.

CHAPTER TEN

As Hot as a Brick

In 1975, Mozambique got its independence from the Portuguese Colonial Master. I can tell you that before this, we used to hear thunders of guns and bombs from the Mozambican side day and night for many past years. We were informed that it was because of the war that had rocked that country for many years.

Mozambique's liberation brought tense and fast changes to my area. The number of the comrades was growing fast. We were now told that boys and girls were now being trained in Mozambique as the ZANLA forces had moved their bases from Zambia, under their chief in command comrade Rex Nhongo. Comrades brought with them the Zimbabwe Magazines in which we learnt the ZANU structure of command. We were told that Comrade Ndabaningi Sithole had sold out, so he was replaced by comrade Robert Garbriel Mugabe the same year (1975).

Through these magazines, we learnt that the guerrilla war in Zimbabwe had started in 1964. We learnt about comrade Joshua Nkomo, comrade Takawira, and comrade Herbert Chitepo whom we were told had just died from a letter bomb in Zambia. He was the first chairman of ZANU (Zimbabwe African National Union). We were told that after some of the ZANLA (Zimbabwe African Liberation Army) forces had been mysteriously been bombarded and killed in Zambia, comrade Ndabaningi Sithole was called as the president to see what had happened to his people. When he arrived, he just instructed for the burial as he was going to America where his son had a headache. This did not go well with the ZANU party. Sithole was sent a letter warning him never to return. That left ZANU party without a leader until they voted for comrade Robert Gabriel Mugabe to take charge in 1975.

Brain storming and conscientisation formed part of our curriculum in the bush. War was part of our lives, we adopted fast, both externally and internally, turning ourselves into fighters as we played it between the two hot sides.

As you have read in the previous sections, both sides were as hot as red hot bricks. We had to survive or die. Well, we chose to survive, so we had to learn how to manage each group without getting burnt. There was no formal school to learn the survival skills. I linked to God. Our school was under the Roman Catholic Church. The Catechist used to come every morning to preach and pray for us before assembly. I felt safe when we were singing the religious songs though I had no idea where that would lead us to. My faith was as shallow as that who just heard there is God.

The other side was the spirit mediums. I had more understanding of this one than religion. This was because our fathers held ceremonies yearly in which the spirit medium (mhondoros) were involved, such as the characteristics of our Shona culture.

I belong to the Chief Makuni dynasty. During the liberation struggle, my grandfather Mr Chinyanda was the chief. I got to know much from him when from 1976 we were forced to settle in clusters, a plan by the Smith regime for them to manage us in their effort to kill the terrorists by starvation as it would be difficult for people to feed them while the Rhodesian army patrolled. Changamire Makuni, as the title for our chief had been since Mambo Dombo's era. He used to tell me our history. He told me the history of our dynasty and the great mhondoros of our clan. He told me secretes of how to become a great leader, which he said was centred on unselfishness and generosity. The only sad story which troubled me till now was when he said to me, "Take a pen and write these things because if I see the end of this Chimurenga War, I will jump the Mukonde Mountains." I did not understand, but he would repeat these words every time we sat down to talk. He used to play his small mbira instrument as he sat on his chair. I used to enjoy listening to the music. I would ask him to play certain songs as I listened attentively. I will tell you more about the late Changamire Makuni later.

In the above passages, I mentioned people being forced to move to settle in clusters in areas chosen by the Smith regime. From 1975, the intensity of the war was getting hotter and painful. Besides losing our relatives into Mozambique, many people were tortured mainly by the Rhodesian soldiers as they attempted to stop people from engaging with the terrorists (comrades).

I recall one day at night, as the whole village was asleep, a big boom! Sound shook our huts. Even the rats that made their homes in the grassed roofs fell. These were two land minds that had been detonated by the two huge trucks carrying many Rhodesian soldiers on their way to Mary Mount Mission where others camped. Within a moment, we heard footsteps and knocks at our doors. These were comrades waking us up to help them carry the heavy guns and ammunition they had, as the mujubhas exchanged with those whom they had taken from the faraway place. This was how we managed transportation of heavy weapons, mujubhas would be assigned a distance from one point to hand over to the group at the next point. Young people like me in my early days, we would be sent to the shops or run fast to the group of comrades at the nearby village to inform them as directed by the comrades in our village. This system worked well and much faster than a telephone.

Strong fathers and boys woke up in that night to carry the weapons as instructed. Soon after they departed, helicopters started hovering above our houses. A bomb was dropped near to our house. The darkness disappeared as they shot their bright canisters to give light. With such light, it would be possible to see even a hare under cover. They searched throughout the night, but the comrades had gone very far away. That morning, the soldiers unleashed a wave of violence against the villagers. My uncle who was about the marriage age, was struck by the buttock of a gun right on the eye and a wound opened up leading to the gashing of lots of blood. This was very stressful in our eyes as young children. Many huts were torched to ashes as well as the food stores, we were left empty. Sometimes cattle were shot and killed as they complained that these were a source of income to feed terrorists. We lost ten of our cattle on that day.

In the early months of 1976, an aeroplane known as a Dakota flew above us with a voice calling for war to cease as they said there was an agreement in a meeting held in Lusaka that the war had ended. The voice encouraged all those who were thinking of joining the terrorists and those terrorists with guns to put their guns down and lift their hands to submit themselves to the nearest camp, as the war had ceased. I could not believe how this could be true as we had just experienced one of the hottest wars those days. After a few days of the Dakota message, the Rhodesian army forced march us to settle some six kilometres away from our area. This was a settlement at the foot of the Mukonde Mountains. Three large villages were grouped together, but families were meant to build their huts according to their headman (sabhuku). This formed the biggest settlement in the Mapinga area which stretched from the foot of Mukonde Mountains down the road to Nyauronzvi River. My mother was given a house by the great Changamire Makuni. That was the time I mentioned earlier, that I used to sit with the great mambo as he told me about our dynasty and the history of our great country Zimbabwe. He told about how people lived before and after the colonial master settled in this beautiful land.

CHAPTER ELEVEN

The Lion Three Meters from my Hut

My father and his brothers had over fifty cattle. We were the richest in terms of cattle the whole settlement. I was fully in charge of the well-being of our cattle as I was the oldest of the boys this time. We used to take them right at the back of the mountains where we would spend the whole day. Lots of activities took place out there. I would like to emphasise the fact that, the mountains were thick so thick that every animal of the forest would be found.

During those days, as I was by myself, looking after our cattle in the tall grass and thick forests, one of my cows got astray, so I began hunting for it. As I was going around through the paths and tall grass, I felt a shower on my leg. Remember, I had not put any trousers on my body by that time, I just had shorts and no shirt in most of the times. Yes, I suddenly stopped and retreated slowly. I knew that could be a huge snake I was encroaching into its territory.

Having concentrated my focus, I came eye to eye with a heap of a huge grey snake in the grass, almost ready to strike as it had made an s-shape with its neck and head. Research proved that whenever a snake is about to strike or spring, it forms an s-shape. They also spit to warn the intruder before striking.

I was face to face with the most dangerous snake known as the black mamba (nyamubobo), which when it strikes you will die within five minutes. The saliva was poisonous too. I knew exactly what to do in such incidents, my grandfather had taught me, that whenever one is bitten by a snake, the best method to slow the poison from circulating the body would be to tie the leg above the affected area, and to keep changing positions after a while to avoid permanent damage to the affected area. Another advice is to reduce active movements; if possible, the person affected should sit and rest while others run around to get help. I decided to tie the top of my thigh and walked home since I was alone. I cautiously walked all the way home and luckily, the great Changamire Makuni was there. He went into one of his hut and brought an old white paper in which some powders were. He took out his sharp razor blade and made small cuts at the spot where I showed him on my leg although the saliva had dried. He put his own saliva on his smallest finger and dipped it into the powder to stick some up, before squeezing the powder into the small cuts he had made on my skin. He looked into my eyes compassionately and reassured me that I was safe. Feeling relieved and life coming back into my heart, I thanked him and left to my mother's house. No negative side effects developed on my leg thereafter.

The day I will never forget was one of the days in winter, the grass was still a mixture of green and golden patches of green and dry grass. The rivers were still flowing, with small streams flowing on the river beds. As usual, I drove my cattle right beyond the mountains. As I walked down the slopes, lazily sliding my feet on the slippery soil, I cast my sight down the low plains, to my surprise, I saw the unusual that afternoon. One of the big trees was covered in a huge white cloth. You could see this from any point because the tree was big and tall. I was curious, so here I was once again. I moved nearby step by step. Remember, this was the middle of a thick forest. Who could have put such a white thing in the middle of such a place? I had many unanswered questions as I pressed on. As curious as a cat, I placed my palm to cover the top of my eye lids intending to have a clear vision. I saw that the big cloth was undulating up and down. Who could have been under this big thing to move it? I did not stop even though fear caged my heart. I could feel the beat of my heart. I pressed on closer and closer as curiosity overcame all. One of my ox was grazing near the tree, so I gained courage. Finally, I touched the beautiful silky cloth, so beautiful my eye had never seen. I tried to tear it, but I could not. I did not know what to do with it. I just left it like that, but questions without answers lingered in my mind throughout the day, whose cloth it was? How did it come there? Where from? The answer finally got my ears from one of the elders from a nearby village whom I met as he cut poles in the forest. He told me that it was a parachute left by the Rhodesian army who had been dropped there one night as they advanced into war against the comrades at the nearby village further that side of the mountain.

Well, that did not disturb my day. Down the stream was an old field in which two of my cows grazed. I decided to go and drive them to join the rest as I was about to go home. As I dashed down the path, I saw a troop of baboons crossing ahead. Some had babies on their backs others red patches on their buttocks. They continued as I watched in amusement. At the back was the biggest of them. This was a very stubborn animal. It walked with pride and slowly. Its tail had a loop before it dropped straight pointing to the ground and it's back curved downwards to form a nice depression. Right in the path it set to face me. My heart started pumping fast. I had my axe. I took two stones and held the handle of my axe like a gun. I started to make some threatening noise as I knocked the stones as if I was shooting at it, but the naughty stubborn animal sat still. This time advancing in short steps. I realised that the war could result me as a looser, then I withdrew backwards as I continued with my threats until I vanished behind the foliage. Watching from afar, the animal disappeared into the valley into the stream and crossed over. Then, hurriedly, I gathered my cows and moved them so fast to join the others which had made their wayward home.

The sun had not completely set at the front point of the mountain, but the trees formed their shadows as they interrupted the rays of light from shining on us. My cattle formed a straight line about half a kilometre long down the path. This surprised me because I would be struggling to file them this way. They seemed shocked to me. Their tails tucked, they moved with speed. I was very happy, so I relaxed right at the back. As we approached the Tsvinje River, I heard a hissing sound on the right side of the path. This was just after the cow in the last end of the queue nearer to me had just passed. There was a four meter gape between. I turned my eyes to see a meandering shinny stretch of a snake advancing as it uncoiled from its paused state. I jumped backwards and stood in fear, shock and curiosity as the grey monster crossed the path, it was about three meters long. I saw it disappearing into the cave deep into the cleft.

I hurriedly followed my cattle only to find them running and pushing each other as they crossed the river. It was a bit darker in the river as the sun had returned into its mother's womb. I happened to look back so as to have a final glimpse of the sun's rays shining on the top most rocks above the cliff behind me. I could not believe what I saw there. My heart leapt out of its cage. I pinched myself to see if I was alive. I swore at myself why I looked there. I asked myself whether this was dreaming or not. A hairy lion was watching us as we passed by the foot of that cliff. I realised why my cattle behaved so differently today. By that time, my cattle were covered in dust as they ran up the mountain with the greatest speed. I tried to catch up with them in vain. Up the mountain they went. As I struggled to increase my speed, it seemed as though I was reversing. Thanks to God, my breath was still in me and I pumped forward against the steep rise. Up the mountain I went. I looked down the other side of the mountain, my cattle still covered in dust, I could only see their backs and horns as they galloped down the slope. I did not slow down as I followed suite. Our village was in sight. I could see and hear people making different noises as they prepared for the coming night. Down the slope I ran, my wish, if I could swallow the distance between me and my mother or had I developed a small engine for acceleration. Sweat oozed out of my body as if I was under heavy rain. Within the shortest time my cattle were in their kraal. I hurriedly closed them in and walked very fast to my mother's house. I did not manage to tell my mother due to shock. Before we finished our supper, the king of the forest roared. It was as if it was at the back of my hut. Some rats were seen running from one hut to another due to shock, so as cockroaches. The king was coming down the mountain.

The whole village retired to bed straight away. I went to bed with two of my cousins in the small hut I had constructed myself. Deep down the night, I heard my door forced open. I briefly died for I did not remember how my mother entered in. She was carrying my little sister who was a baby in her hands. "Shiii! Listen!" My mother whispered to us. We heard some funny and indescribable sounds. She continued, "Those are two lions about three meters behind this hut feasting on a cow they have been chasing and killed. I heard how they chased and killed it." There was a dead silence in the hut as fear engulfed us. Only the cutting, tearing and swallowing sounds as the lions feasted upon their kill. "Pwaaaa! Krrrrrrr! Grugrugrugru! Gujugujuguju!" went the sounds. We could hear their heavy breathing and belching in that darkness. Thoughts encroached my brain cells, imagining if that chewing was my head or my bones. Gradually, I was beginning to hallucinate. However, the presents of my mother kept me alive. "Stay in hear," She ordered us to stay indoors as she was going to inform elders at my grandmother's compound. I swore in my heart that I would not allow her to take such a risk. I jumped at the door, and got stuck by the door so as to block her from opening it, little did I know that mum could lift me into the air and safely put me aside like a baby. She did this without any sign of struggle. Naked as I was, she lifted me as I tried to resist tangling in the air crying silently as she put me aside to make her way out. She opened the door and left with my sister in her hands. They disappeared into the dark.

We retired to our beds where we covered ourselves under our blankets as the only salvation.

Within a short spun of time, the elders were out with fire and drums as they shouted. This was to scare the lions away. The following morning, we had to share the remnants of the dead cow. What a close shave?

CHAPTER TWELVE

A Week as a
Prisoner of War

The war raged on. Between 1977 and 1979 we saw the cruellest war on the land. More and more boys and girls were still crossing over to Mozambique to be trained and returned to fight the enemy back home. Within a few months of training, they would be ready. The number of the comrades multiplied so fast such that it was possible to meet them whichever village you visited.

We continued to go to school as we played active double roles. The Rhodesian army brought a message to our parents. They told them not to kill and eat any sick domestic animal. We did not know they had injected viruses to kill all our animals, but no one understood how. We used to take our animals to the dip every year where they would be treated by injections and dipping in the dip tank. Information from the Rhodesian Army followed the day after they had compulsorily ordered everyone to take their cattle to the dip. They said they were preventing an outbreak of a tick born disease which could have wiped out our cattle if we did not. Our cattle perished. This was the most painful part in my life as we witnessed our animals parting in a very sad manner. I remember one day, my father and I went to the kraal as we intended to yoke two oxen for ploughing. I opened the kraal's entrance and went straight to hold the horns of one which was still resting in the mud. I put the rope around its horns then I stretched my hand to hold the horns of the other which was resting nearby and did the same. Calling their names to rise but they could not move. To me they were just being lazy to stand in that morning, so I called my father to help. He hurriedly came in with his whip. He was the one to notice that the two were dead in their sleep. They just froze in their sleeping positions. We dug big pits by their sides and buried them in. Most of them all died the same way. We did not benefit from our forty to fifty cattle I suffered to look after all those years.

After the death of our cattle, I became free to play with my age group boys. We used to do quite a lot of activities during the war, as we had trained ourselves to enjoy life to the fullest as we knew it could end any time. We played children's games in which we would group with youths from other villages to play drums and music. We could even compete against each other. In our area, we had many skilled young boys who played drums skilfully. One such a boy was named Mishack Chiweshe, he topped them all.

Christmas celebrations were characterised by various entertaining games. The popular Chimuzokoto, Dandi, Mbira, Mafuwe, Makwingwindo, occupied our minds to the point of forgetting that we were at war. Sometimes comrades were part of the crowds as they joined in with their own styles of celebrations. They enjoyed music from their radio grams.

One bright night as we were playing Zairian and Kenyan rhumba music under the baobab tree, boys and girls mixed with the comrades as they showed different styles of jiving. Those days bump jive was in fashion. This happiness was suddenly ended by the mhondoro, spirit medium who called the leader of the comrades, by the name comrade Magogo, to advise them to be cautious as they had seen Rhodesian soldiers just a kilometre away. The mhondoro advised everyone to sit quietly as they intended to blindfold them. Suddenly the village was as silent as a graveyard. We just slept alongside the walls of the huts like that. The following morning, our dear comrades left towards the direction of the Mukonde Mountains, while their enemy soldiers walked into the village from the other end. They told our village headman that they had seen all what happened during the night. "We came as close as hundred meters away and used our binoculars to view," said the commander. One of them asked the headman where the terrorists had gone, to which the headman quickly pointed to the mountains and said, "Look there, they are! Follow them and stop asking silly questions". Our head man was a very courageous man; he used to speak to both groups without fear. The commander just gave a laugh before ordering his men to leave the headman alone. They took the opposite direction, where they had left their trucks.

The other game I enjoyed during the war was going fishing. Our dam was about five kilometres from the village. One of the biggest dams in my area that time known as Mukonde Dam, was situated in the western end of the Mukonde Mountains on the Nyamakamba River. Boys and girls used to use various methods of fishing in the

waters of this dam. I used the fishing line and its hook. That day
we had agreed to go fishing as a group. It was just the onset of the
winter season in 1978. The sun was partially covered in clouds
and the ground was not too dry as a film of moisture covered the
top soil. Our foot prints could open the moistened soil to expose
the dry soil below as we strode along the road to the dam. I was
as excited as we joked throughout the journey. My worms were in
my mother's small tea pot as I carefully tucked it under my armpit.
We did not take long before we took our positions in the water. I
decided to settle among the reeds as I moved a bit deeper in the
water. Most of my colleagues went to parade on the dam-wall as they
started to enjoy the catch. Their position of choice was strategic in
that they could see all around the corners of the pool. However,
my chosen position was covered all around by the reeds and other
water plants. I was so absorbed into catching the fish not aware
that my colleagues had already disappeared behind the wall and ran
away home. No one of them warned me that there were Rhodesian
soldiers coming from the far end of the dam. One of the boys who
had been warned passed behind me as he shouted to me to come
out quickly, since the soldiers had almost arrived. It took me time to
rush out of water and start my way running. "Stop! Stop!" the voice
came. When I turned, I saw one of the soldiers pointing his gun at
me ready to shoot. I dropped my fishing line and put my hands in
the air to surrender. The big, hairy, tall and fierce soldier advanced
towards me as I stretched my hands further in the air. Gripped in
fear, I thought they were not seeing me well so, with my eyes wide
open, I stood on my toes and kept on stretching my body up with
my fingers pointing to the sky. I wished I could grow taller than
everything around. The tall huge white soldier stood above my
head. His face was covered in beard and his nostrils were like two
pairs of exhausts ready to draw me in. I could hear his breath. I did

not have the courage to look at him twice as I collapsed and fainted. All what followed was just like a dream. He spoke in English, but I could just hear the words 'father and Mozambique'. He held one of my short's buckles which I used to hold my short tight on me and hackled me tangling in the air before he drew his bayonet out. When I had a glimpse of this sharp knife, I passed out. He cut the metallic head of my buckle and I dropped to the ground like a pawpaw from a tall tree. "Buu!" I dropped, landing on the stony ground with my left side. I felt numb and painful, but who cared? There was no one to cry to. Baba vakanditengera kuSalisbury, (my father bought it for me from Salisbury), I continued to tell him in Shona that the short was bought from the city by my father as I thought he was accusing me of buying it from Mozambique.

He ordered me to rise and walk to the road. I hurriedly gathered myself and timidly followed them. As we walked, I realised that there was another boy of about seventeen years who had also been caught up in the raid. I was just about eleven to twelve years old when they took me onto their truck which was packed with fierce and armed soldiers. There were two fully packed army trucks. I knew well that if the comrades ambushed us, they would not spare my life as the kill would supersede my life. My colleague was put in the other truck and both of us were ordered to stand to act as human shields. They drove with us along the Mozambique—Zimbabwe boarder road. Through the most notorious forests where we could easily be bombed, we penetrated up the dark streams and forests. Behind the unknown mountains the trucks rolled. In those thick forests, they stopped their trucks and all jumped out in all directions. We remained in the trucks as they wracked doors and burnt houses as well as shooting and killing domestic animals, mercilessly. I remained sitting on the truck, and I had no idea where we were. Fortunately the villagers had deserted their homes well before the trucks arrived. No arrests were made on this raid. It took about an hour before they packed themselves and started out on journey again.

The drive was not easy because the roads were so poor. Sometimes it would appear as if the trucks would pour us out as they rolled over big stones on the road. The trucks swerved and meandered along the dusty and narrow road. One moment, I had a feeling that my death was creeping near due to the gun barrel of that huge soldier squeezed my leg. The two vehicles rolled on and on. After about two hours of drive, we finally came to a camp which I later realised to be at Mary Mount Mission. I had never been at this place in my life and I did not know the direction home. We were ordered to get down and join other war prisoners who were there.

We found that there were over twenty war prisoners in the camp. We were to live packed in the same fashion like the slave ship carrying slaves across the Atlantic Ocean from Africa in a three sided walled structure. On the floor was a dirty green tent which was alive with very big lice. Some of the lice had tails. They had dark red colour of the blood they sucked day and night. That was my first time to set my sight on tailed lice. Some parts of the tent had spatter dash if blood from the crushed lice. I designed a mass distraction weapon with my fingers in which I could crash multiple number of lice with a single crash.

During the night, we could not sleep because of the bugs that sucked out our blood. Sometimes the bugs would feast upon our backs as we sat against the walls with our legs par to the floor. There was a bug, we named the night raider. These were maggots which came out at night. With their pointed fronts they easily dug into our flesh before syphoning the blood into their cylindrical bodies. They were huge and easy to hold and crash as we would be asleep, leaving blood sports everywhere on the tent.

The structure was smaller than the number of occupants, so we had to sleep in radial formation. I slept next to a conical metallic bucket placed in the corner nearest to the right side of the entrance. Our toilet was that bucket. This is where we used to urinate and defecate too. Early in the morning, we would carry the overflowing bucket to offload into pits outside the fence under guard by an armed soldier. I did carry this bucket one of the days, but as a young boy, the staff spilled and flowed down my body. After emptying the buckets in small pits, we would clean it and put some beans to cook. The cooked beans we poured onto the dish before we used the same bucket to cook sadza. So was the cruel prison life. I suffered the smell and the splashes of urine and faeces on my bedding area.

One afternoon, a black soldier named Shereni came to our shelter and hand-picked me to follow him to his tent. I was so afraid, but I strengthened myself. I followed him like a dog following its cruel master to his tent. My head was boiling, with thoughts I could not understand. One thought dominated was, that was a journey to my destination. "Come in young boy!" He called me in. "Hold this cabinet door boy and be steady right!" He ordered me to hold the door of his cabinet which he was fixing. As I held, he missed the whole because I was visibly shivering with fear. This upset him and he warned me with a harsh voice, "Boy! Be careful! Be stable!" This made my fear worse than before. He slapped me on my right eye so hard that I saw stars, however, I calmed myself for a moment as he successfully slotted the screw. He ordered me to return back to the prisoners' shelter.

As I hurriedly paced towards the shelter, I was horrified with what I heard and saw. On my left side before I turned towards our shelter, was a tree under which was a small structure built of zinc sheets. Above this structure was one of the branch of the tree on which a chain hung into the small structure which could accommodate three to four men. No one could suspect any mischiefs in that structure. It was a depressing voice which came from the small structure which attracted my attention. It was a voice seeking for liberation, a cry for life. The voice, which I failed to describe nor to tell which animal it was coming from. "Yooo weee amaaii!" I heard it louder as it disappeared into that structure, it went low and died off. Suddenly a demanding and commanding voice enquired, "Talk! Where are the terrorists? Are you not one of them?" I heard a sharp sound as if a cruel rodeo man troubled a stubborn hoarse. There was no answers to these demands.

As I stood with curiosity, I saw through a small slit which gave me a clear picture about what was happening in there. I saw one of the man who slept on my left side in our shelter last night. His legs were up, held by the chains which hung from the tree. His head was down above a big drum full of water. He hung there like a cow to be slaughtered before it's skinned off. One of the huge beard white soldier held the other end of the chain. He was the one who was holding the life of that helpless man in his hand. As the soldier pulled the chain, the man got lifted up above the drum. That was the moment I could hear his distressed wailing. When the soldier let the chain slowly, the poor man's cry could not be describable till the voice died off. It was a horrific scene. I pinched myself just to make sure I was alive and seeing reality. I did not know how to help that man. My question was, why did I see these things? Was there anything I could do to help? No one answered. Like a rat soaked in water all night long, I staggered towards the shelter, I told no one till today, as I write to the world. All day and night, I waited to see that man, who slept alongside me the previous nights, to return, but, up to now, he never returned. They might have torched him till death. But, where did they burry him? No one knows up to now. So was the struggle for independence in Zimbabwe. Many people disappeared just like that. The ZANU PF's Mugabe government never bothered to investigate or to help the poor orphans left behind. The wind just blew it away.

I spent seven days under these conditions. I had no idea what this meant. However, the morning of the eighth day, two white soldiers came to the tent and pointed at me to pack and go home. I could not believe it. What I remembered was that I found myself running very fast, in the direction I was not sure to be leading to my village. I did not bother to ask how I could get home, as I feared they might hold me back. Down the road I ran for my life. The further I went the more I ran. I thought they were following me. I trotted and ran till I was about ten kilometres away. I then began to think, which direction was home? I was tired, sweating, thirsty, and hungry. I saw a baobab tree under which I went to pick some baobab fruits and started to break and eat. I continued to walk down the road before I came across any village. I crossed a river and pressed up the slope, when miraculously, I saw a moving figure ahead. Closer and closer the figure became clearer that it was a man on his bicycle. I stopped the man to ask how I could find my way to my primary school, Nyamanyanya. Most places are named after a school so I knew it would be easy to identify schools than other places. The man told me to continue with the road until I got to the school. He estimated the distance left to be about five more kilometres. I gave thanks and tirelessly walked along that road until I came to Mukuhununu Dam. This was where we used to dip our cattle and to collect water before we were moved to the new settlement. I knew this area. My heart opened with joy and relief as I took the right way home. I took the way to my school where I would begin my journey home. Over the river, I saw my school, I felt really at home. However, from the school to my village was another ten kilometre journey. It was just past the noon clock, when I started the journey from my school home. I walked till I could not see the school behind me. I started to think where my mother could be at that time. To the fields, was my answer? Then I swung myself to the fields which were beyond the mountains. I walked fast up the bushy mountains beyond and down the slopes I went. I peeped through the trees below to see our field which stretched from the foot of the mountain. I was very excited and imagined how my mother would feel to see me. I imagined holding my mother and to see her beautiful smile again. By this time, I had just set my feet on the edge of the field. Right across the field I saw them, I looked with my palm over my eyes, and I identified my mother as they worked on the field. I walked courageously towards them. I saw my mother, standing straight, looking at me. She moved side by side and moved step by step and used her palm to get a clear vision. I saw her dropping what she was holding and started to trot across the field. She tried to speed, but her legs held her and stumbled almost fell, but she continued faster. I was running towards her and we met in the middle of the field where she snatched me from the ground and held me firmly against her chest. I had never been held so comfortable in my mother's hands like that before. She gave me the kiss that I will not forget as tears oozed out of her eyes and she continued to thank God all the way. On the other hand, I was crying emotionally. My sisters came and embroiled me as they cried with jubilation. My mother gave me some food and ordered all of us to return home in happiness. She slaughtered her biggest rooster as a welcome home for me.

Surely, the Chimurenga War almost swallowed me. What a near miss?

CHAPTER THIRTEEN

Tough Hearts

The life style and surrounding circumstances we grew in by this moment, produced tough, fearless and courageous boys who were prepared to face any form of challenges without neither the fear of defeat nor death. Young and old, grew up to be united and learnt to work and fight challenges in unity. If one of us was affected in one way or another, the whole village would know within the shortest space of time and everybody would feel equally the same. There was no sympathy, but empathy. Together with our wise parents and extended families were like the colours of the rainbow. It was not easy to identify whose child or parent for whom.

Some of the boys were far more courageous than others resulting in them becoming leaders of groups. Others waited till ideas turned into meaningful activities. Hunting was one activity boys enjoyed doing. Some used nets to catch wild animals, others used dogs and sometimes snares.

Here is one occasion in which my cousin Oliver proved his tough heartedness. One autumn warm day, he decided to go hunting alone. He collected his five dogs and disappeared into the mountains. The reader should always remember the characteristics of our mountains and forests. These were alive with all types of wild animals, and plants. One could not predict what he or she could come across in those bushes, so they entered in at their own risk. Oliver and his dogs had just been swallowed by the thick forest. He was a young boy aged fourteen, short but tough in stature. His cuffs were short and round as if he had packs of tennis balls in them. His body was characterised by lines of blood vesicles and muscles which intertwined all over his arms. A round headed boy with wide, sharp and prominent eyes. His skin colour was light brown than most of the boys in the village. This was the boy, alone deep into the ferocious forests of the Nyamanyanya Mountains. His dogs were well trained. They knew how to hunt in such forests. As soon as they entered the forests, they scattered in all directions sniffing all the bushes and grass. They had made a history of being able to trace an animal even if it had passed through a week before. They made different warning sounds whenever they encountered something. They could fight a lion together. These were the type of dogs Oliver had.

The young boy went forwards, sideways and sometimes in circles in his bid to sniff out a kudu or a buck. He decided to cross the river Nyamakamba, up the hill he went. In his hand was his axe. Suddenly he heard his dogs barking. They sounded to have been afraid. Oliver ran courteously, his eyes wide open, viewing sideways like a binocular. To his perplex, he saw a leopard almost jumping at him from the tree above. He leapt aside, like a cat on a hot brick, and landed on a stone which made him to stagger, losing the grip of his axe in the process. He did not have the chance to pick his axe as he was under attack by the killer leopard. It struck his back with its claws causing tear and scratches on his skin. He swung to the left then swiftly turned to confront the animal which had turned to attack his dogs as they had surrounded it. The fearless boy grabbed the beast's tail and began to dance with it. Great grandfather had taught us that the power of any tailed animal is in its tail, so as the leopard tried to turn to the left, Oliver jerked to the right, very hard, whichever direction the animal moved, he pulled its tail in the opposite direction. His hold gave chance for the dogs to attack the beast. They had surrounded it one in front, two on its left side and the other two on the right while Oliver anchored on its tail. The battle raged on for about an hour. The leopard tried to stand on its hind legs, so as to enable its front claws work upon the dogs. Oliver new well that given slightest opportunity, the leopard's front paws could terminate his dog's lives, and so he dragged and lifted the tail as soon as it posed that way. His dogs behaved like the army of ants. They attacked from their sides simultaneously, as if there was a referee. They tore into its rib cage, pulling the colourful skin off. It was losing blood on each side of its stomach. This reduced its energy and ability to fully get into combat. Eventually, the killer was made to sleep forever. They had killed a very big male leopard which must have been one of the killers of our goats. It was a very beautiful animal with black and white spots all over its skin.

Oliver laid it in the centre as he sat on a stone checking how seriously he had been hurt. On his back, were four shallow lines running down the back. The blood that came out had dried leaving red lines. He had no other injuries. His dogs sat around the dead animal as they punted with their tongues out. Oliver checked on all of them some had cuts on their skins but one had its belly opened showing the intestines out, this later died and he buried the courageous animal in a cave.

After burying his dog, he pulled the leopard and hide it in another cave where he covered it with branches of small bushes. He left, and took his way home to tell the elders to take the dead animal home.

The village people sang songs of praise and glorified the courageous boy. The leopard was carried home on two strong poles by four big and strong men. What a fearless boy Oliver was?

Fearlessness can be so dangerous such that one can easily be attacked to death without attempting to run away from danger. Five to six years had passed after Oliver and his dogs had killed the leopard. One afternoon as the sun cooled down. My three cousins younger than me and I decided to go to the river to have a bath after the day's work in the fields. We decided to follow the unclear path in the tall grass. The grass covered all our heights. We formed a single file down the slope. As the oldest, I lead the group. Chatting, joking and laughing as we paved the way down. I was putting on one of my trousers that day. We pressed down as we got closer to the river; I suddenly felt a cold feeling from my ankle up my right leg to the hips. I stood still. Everybody stopped since I was in lead. I realised what had got into my trousers. Without moving my legs, I used my hands to press very hard and squeezed the head together with my trousers on my hips to take out life of whatever was in. I did this with accuracy and precision such that I had no doubt whatever my fingers crashed was destroyed.

I then shook my trousers from the hip downwards in order to remove whatever was in. I lifted my leg, only to find a pile of a snake dropping from my trousers. When they saw this, my cousins began running away. I just stood to laugh at them. I taught them a lesson that if I had panicked, the snake could have made several bites on my leg. They were speechless to my behaviour. We buried the snake in a hole and pressed on.

As all these events took place, the war of liberation raged on.

My mother was brave too. Way back in 1976, at dusk, I had just arrived from the cattle kraal. Soon after opening the door to our kitchen as I intended to quench my thirst, I heard a voice calling from the nearby bush, "My young brother! Hey young man! Come here! Do not be afraid, we are your brothers, come closer." I looked intensively, but I could hardly see anything until the bush started to move. I realised that these were the comrades. I consciously walked towards the bush. There was a man holding a gun. His head covered in leaves as a hat. He lovingly greeted me and requested for a cup full of water, which I happily and speedily provided. He requested for a digging hoe which I did not resist to let go. He disappeared into the foliage. I realised these guys were up to something serious.

Two to three hours had passed, darkness had settled upon the land. I had already told my mother about the man I had seen. She in turn warned, us to expect anything that night. The main road was three quarters of a kilometre away from our houses. Just before we retired to bed, we heard sounds of vehicles from far away towards the direction of the notorious Mary Mount Camp. The sound grew louder and louder as the trucks approached the bridge nearest to our village. As they slowed down to negotiate the steep slopes, we heard, "Booom! Pwaaaaa! Trrrrrrraaaaa! Packpackpack! Shiiiiii pwiyooooo! Popopopopopopop! Mviiiiimviiiiimviiii!" stray bullets crossed above us. This went on for about twenty minutes. We all kept flat on the ground.

A blind silence followed this deafening noise. I pinched myself and found that I was still alive. My mother collected my two sisters, one on her hands and the toddler she held by hand. She ordered me to follow behind as she speedily walked with us into the bush. I had no idea where mother was taking us at that time in the dark. I just followed knowing well that I was well protected by the great mother. I knew for sure nothing could harm us as long as my mother was with us.

The darkness swallowed us. She led us through the thick forests and rocks, the direction of the headman's field in which he killed the python. We could hear the hyenas laughing and giggling. Wild dogs sounded as they gathered on hunting missions. A leopard coughed from the rocky hill on our right side. I was mixed up, fear and drowsiness haunted me. My mother braved on. She targeted one of the baobab trees which was well known for its hollow trunk which was used by people to hide from rain. Little did I know she was taking us into this mighty tree's womb for our bedroom that night? She threw us in one by one before she climbed in. She did not sleep throughout the night as we slept peacefully our heads on her legs. I dreamt being in a warm soothing bed all night long. It was as comfortable as new bed.

Just before dawn, my mother picked me and threw me outside, she did the same to all my sisters, one by one, before she jumped out. My heart pumped faster and faster soon after I beheld leopard's and hyena's foot prints on the entrance. Questions of fear lingered in my mind. What if these dangerous animals had jumped in? How would my mother going to fight them? I looked at her face with love, encouragement and pride of this courageous woman, who kept us safe all the night from marauding wild animals. I smiled at her, exposing all the teeth in the front of my mouth. I had never brushed them since the loss of my milk teeth. Mum led us to the fields where we spent the whole day. In the evening, she safely took us back home. We got home to find everything intact. I would not blame mother for what she had done, as events were unpredictable when such type of war occurred. What a brave woman my mother was?

CHAPTER FOURTEEN

The Death of the Great Chief (Changamire) Makuni

The year 1978 was declared the year of the people by the ZANLA forces under the leadership of Comrade Josiah Magama Tongogara as chief of defence. In this year, comrades drilled the mass about how to avoid death in the event of open fire encounters. They warned that the year 1979 would be the year of the storm in which the enemy would be attacked wherever he would be. It was therefore imperative for people to know how to survive under any war situation. The roads were full of land mines and we were no longer setting our feet along them as we resorted to the bush paths. The war got hottest near the end of the year 1978. I remember one day, a land mine was detonated by the army truck as they tried to pull back from the notorious camp at Mary Mount Mission. We were in the base in one of the mountains when the comrades dispatched three of the boys Richard, Charles and Thomas to go and check the effectiveness of the land mine. The boys set their journey through the forest parallel to the main road. On their way, they broke into argument. Richard and Charles opting to walk along the road as Thomas resisted. Charles walked close to the edges of the road while Richard went to the centre of the road; Thomas remained in the bush some meters from the road. They walked on, across the river up the river they went. Suddenly, "Boom!" a land mine thundered. Richard had stepped it, nothing of him was buried. Charles was buried in pieces. Thomas got his skin burnt but he found himself running aimlessly away into the bush. He was discovered the following day alive but confused. He recovered well to tell this story. Today, he built his house close to this site.

What a loss, vibrant lives got lost just like that? So was the Second Chimurenga War from which today such greatest fighters have been forgotten. These were the heroes who made us independent. They acted like water and the comrades like fish. What life would fish have without water? Which one is greater? Would the comrades fight the war and win without these suffering people? Today our ZANU (PF) has totally forgotten us. We still bleed. Not yet healed since thirty-two years ago today as we mark our nation's thirty second birth day. When shall it be? War collaborators have not been rewarded.

The war raged on. It almost took me to the graves one day. The Rhodesian army entered our village from the lower end of the big compound. I was busy whistling as I perfected the new axe handle I was making under the cool shade of the mighty baobab tree. Swiftly came one of the boys running like a headless chicken, he did not notice me as he ran towards the stream that meandered at the edge of the villages. He disappeared to my amazement. This set my heart pound like a hungry mother pounding the only meal of the day. When I cast my eyes from where the boy came from, I jumped like a cat on hot bricks. What I realised was that within incalculable time, I was running ahead of that boy towards the mountains. Knowing well that we would be visible since we were up the slope and the soldiers down, we ran down the stream. The problem was that the stream meandered downward towards the enemy direction. We had to go flat on our bellies like snakes until we were out of the danger zone. When I stood behind the acacia tree, I realised that my leg was bleeding profusely. The left lower limb had opened from the knee down the front to the ankle. I did not feel pain. We peeped through the thick forest to get a glimpse of the village, my eyes could not see as the whole village was on fire. I could hear gunshots too. Some lost houses and the food stored in and others lost their live stocks. The wind swept the whole village within half an hour all was done. Fires bellowed as smoke connected earth to the clouds. People had spread in all directions in attempt to save their lives. Thank God, not even one person was killed in this marauding raid. The soldier enemy left our village whipping and coughing. Our silos were burnt so as my mother's house. So was the war, we were getting used to this. It was impossible to account for the losses.

Weeks later, the land was engulfed by a new version of war in which chiefs were being killed by the comrades. They were accused of delaying the liberation by conniving with the Rhodesian government. I did not believe this theory up to now as most people believed it was propaganda by the comrades. How could chiefs like my grandfather do that? He played a very big role to ensure that the lives of our dear comrades were safe. He was the corner stone of the society, encouraging unity among his people to care for each other.

He fed the poor, he loved everyone and he was a humble kind man with his people at heart. The war formed his day to day activities. He kept tools which the comrades took to use as they planted land minds. He provided food and his goats and cattle for meat to the comrades. Chiefs just fell to be the victims of circumstance. Also remember, the chieftainship is passed on among the eligible houses. The next house would benefit out of the death of the current chief. Chiefs became the targets.

One night it was so dark that you could hardly see your back, as I sat by the fire with my grandfather. Comrade Sadza and comrade Satan arrived with their group. We had just heard that chief Rusambo had just been killed by the comrades. The group arrived and ordered to have a meeting with the chief and his circle of counsellors as well as the spirit medium. This was in 1979 in January. The meeting took the whole night. The comrades were warned against their plan by the spirit medium. They were told this would expose all the people to attack by the enemy. The comrades said they would return as they left.

That time, I had over seven of my goats which my father slaughtered to feed the comrades. All the animals were slaughtered one by one as the comrades demanded for meat. That was the time I had left to live with my uncle at my mother's place. One morning, while I was there, a group of mujubhas arrived in the area. One of them told me that Changamire Chinyanda Makuni was no more. He told me that the comrades had ordered the mujubhas, fathers and comrades to dig a grave and they threw my grandfather alive before they pounded him with stones as he cried calling the name of his elder son who eventually succeeded him. They said he was not dead when they ordered people to cover his body with soil. They said he was raising his head and calling, the more they crushed his head. My great grandfather had foretold that he would jump the Mukonde Mountains if he saw the end of the chimurenga war. It was now clear in my mind that he was foretelling about his death. They murdered him in the cruellest manner anyone could imagine. We remember him and all those murdered without blame all over Zimbabwe. Rest in peace garland soldiers. War showed no justice.

The mass got baked from both sides. There was nowhere to run to. The people you were serving could kill instantly. This was a very challenging part of the struggle. Many perished without cause. However, the war heated hotter.

CHAPTER FIFTEEN

Going to Salisbury

After losing everything to say the least, homes, relatives, domestic animals, and the constant smelling of death, I felt it was the end of life. There was no future in my life. No, not even the new Zimbabwe, in which we were promised to be the inheritance of all the aeroplanes, the army trucks even the Dakotas which we had been promised to be the transport means for the mujibhas and chimbwidos by the dear comrades. I thought the new Zimbabwe would be dark and miserable. By the way, by December 1978, our area had declared self-styled independence. It was a no go area for Rhodesian army. There were no cars on the deadly roads. Not even the Rhodesian army vehicles could use the roads. They resorted to air raids. Air raids brought a blanket of misery over our land. The enemy resorted the use of jets. Many people lost lives in such type of war fare. Jets were very fast and swift in action. They travelled faster than their sounds. In most cases, before we heard the sound, the place would be ablaze. Fire would be everywhere and death the characteristic. Not even the trained comrades could escape the bombs. Many innocent living organisms lost lives. It was mass distraction in real sense. 'I must leave this death trap by any means, the sooner the better', I thought so day in day out.

How fast? What means? These were tough questions to answer because travelling to Salisbury was difficulty. People would walk for many kilometres to Rushinga where they could be carried on tractors or private cars to Mt Darwin where buses from Salisbury stopped. A total distance of about 100km.

The war had reached its climax that time spilling into 1979. After the death of Changamire Makuni, many comrades, mujibhas, and chimbwidos died in air raids. I remember the bombing of over two hundred comrades at Nyamudzarumbu and Mudyaturombo villages. We lost quite a number of our friends. Our fathers had to dig big trenches to bury the dead. In my reflection, the warning by the mhondoro that day when they foretold of misery and deaths if the comrades proceeded with their plan to kill the great Changamire, became a reality.

Many people turned against each other and started selling to both comrades and the Rhodesian army, resulting in many unnecessary deaths. The same was about to happen to me. I could feel that some of my nearest relatives did not want me to investigate about the way my goats got killed to feed the comrades. They hatched a plan to do away with me. Had it not been my grandmother who in her own wisdom advised me to run away to Salisbury, I could have perished. I did not argue with my grandmother, so I set on my journey to Salisbury in February 1979.

My cousin and I set on the long journey by feet to Rushinga. Although my cousin had a bicycle, he could not use it since we used the thorny paths in the bush. Very early in the morning before the sun set we started our journey, knowing very well about the curfew which was in place in the area. We could have easily been short dead if we were found out of the village outside the hours according to the law.

It took us two days to get to Rushinga as we had to put up at my cousin's in-laws' place the first night. By mid-day of the second day, we were in a private small blue car on our way to Mt Darwin. On our way, we drove past a freshly detonated land mine which had turned a huge truck with its contents into small pieces of metals flung into tree tops. Our driver seemed to know his wheel pretty well. He reassured us of our safety. Throughout the sixty kilometre journey, people were mum. I wondered what went on in each one's mind. The car could not keep silent, as it rolled up and down the undulating and winding road. I wished if I could swallow the journey ahead. When would we get to our destination? I whispered to my cousin. He did not move, he was like a statue. His eyes wide open and focused at the front of the car as if he was the driver. I grinned at him with a fake smile with the intention of attracting his attention, but his neck was ridged. Maybe it was shock which gripped him. I decided to go my way. I did not enjoy.

It took us less than two hours to get to Mt Darwin bus station. The Uzumba Bus Services was parked and ready to roll its way to Salisbury.

I was very excited to travel by bus for the first time to Salisbury. Going to Salisbury for the first time caused such excitement that I pinched myself several times as I asked whether I was really the one doing so. Sitting by the window watching the moving trees was amazing as the big house speeded. Sometimes I could turn my head and eyes feeling dizzy with excitement. The bus roared up and down the rivers and mountains, up along the meandering road. I wished this could be the way life was. I did not bother about people on the bus as I enjoyed myself throughout the journey. It took us about four hours from Mt Darwin to Salisbury that time. But today, it only takes two hours to cover the same journey.

We got off at Marlborough Police Station and started on our journey down the Salisbury drive now Harare drive to the right side of the great Mazowe Road. I cannot well describe what I saw and how I felt as we strode on the tar mark for the first time. The air I breathed smelt fresh and nice. The beautiful houses and green well cared for lawns surrounded the streets and houses. I was fascinated by the traffic lights, I discovered that they changed automatically, I asked my cousin, who changed them? He just smiled at me. I did not care what went on in his mind. What mattered most was that I was now in Salisbury the great city we used to call Misodziyebere (hyena's tears), in attempt to pronounce the name Salisbury. as we could not clearly pronounce it way back home. There were many cars, buses, bicycles and people walking on feet. I had not seen such, all my life. The beautiful Manyopora shopping centre with its chain of stores, was a marvel to watch. The shops were fully packed with lots of new things. There were so many white people all over. This fascinated me such that I could look at one of them without blinking until he or she was out of sight. What a place to be in? We continued down the road until we turned down Princess Margret Road. We continued down to the last street to the left until we got into number 23 Burrows Close. That was the place where my brother Lazarus was working as a cook to a white family. I was extremely excited to reunite with my brother after a long separation. This became my new home until he lost the job later that year.

CHAPTER SIXTEEN

Independence

Arrival into the sunshine city changed the way I perceived life.
There were neither more bombs nor comrades. Everyone seemed
to be engaged in their own way, and not even to worry about the
war. People heard about the war and what was going on around
the country from the radios and newspapers. Most of the boys and
girls who had fled to the cities enjoyed listening to the radios in bid
to understand more about current affairs. One would marvel to
the way they articulated and debated facts about Zimbabwe, Africa
and the world at large. You would think that Comrade Mugabe was
already the ruler of the country. Talking about Uganda and how Idi
Amin preyed upon his population was sad news to listen. These
guys were well informed and connected to the world I never knew
it existed. Such activities injected new and fresh life in many people
who had been broken down by the war in the rural areas and made
life enjoyable once more. The only sad feelings of missing friends
and relatives in the war zones, remained a knife stuck in the heart.

I missed my mother and sisters which caused me to sob whenever I was alone.

Brother Lazarus got me a Grade 7 place at Glenara Estates Primary School to pursue education. The journey from Marlborough to Glenara School was about eight or more kilometres. This did not deter me from going to school as I began yet another struggle for education. Travelling to and from school was not easy, as I had to walk most of the days. Initially, I had no shoes, which made it very painful to walk on the tar as my feet got worn off by the tar and sometimes got prickled by small stones. I continued going to school anyhow.

May I point out that, even though I mentioned of not having comrades as it was back home, there was curfew in Harare. This posed a big risk to me since I needed to start my journey to school earlier and arrive home before sunset. People could be easily get shot and killed if seen walking in the streets outside the time outlined. One of my home boy was shot dead by his boss as he walked into the compound in Marlborough Drive that time.

I was determined to pursue my studies. My brother was very supportive. I thanked him for the plan to send me to school even though it was tough.

The same year, events were gradually turning nuts in Salisbury; there were reports of comrades being sighted hiding in some of the places in the city. It did not take time before the oil tanks were bombed. This sent a wave of shock to the whole country. The fire was so huge such that South African aircrafts had to be hired to try to put the fire off. This event was followed by the Lancaster House

Conference in London which resulted in a cease fire. I recall, close to the end of the year 1979, comrade Rex Nhongo spoke on the Rhodesia Broadcasting Corporation. In his words he said, "To all freedom fighters, I urge you to keep your weapons and go to the nearest camp identified. Please don't hinder!" That was the day I learnt the new word, "hinder". This marked the cease fire.

Comrades began to make camps around the country. In Harare, we received new guests from Mozambique. A number of houses were identified to accommodate members of the central committee and high command. Close to my house, was comrade Teurai Ropa Joyce Mujuru, another side was comrade Kumbirai Kangai and on the other was comrade Emerson Munangagwa.

Each house had few more comrades to guide them and some young boys and girls who resided with them. We used to do rallies in these houses. I became very active once again because whatever we were doing was similar to what we did back home. I used to lead in singing and talking about war. I later on became more involved in voter education. As a school going pupil, I was the artist in drawing pictures of the symbols on the voting paper. I also campaigned for ZANU around Marlborough and at school. I had moved to Alpha Brick School in Mt Hampden as I repeated Grade Seven since my brother had no money to send me to Secondary School. I had to repeat Grade 7 at my own risk.

In April my brother lost his job. This meant I also lost my home. I had to stay with my cousin who was just about two roads away. My cousin was very kind although things were not as good for him. Because his Boss did not like to see friends and relatives, I did hide and seek. I would leave home very early in the dark hours of the morning without having anything to eat; spent the whole day at school and returned in the night, sometimes after everyone had gone to bed. The mango tree close to his Boss's house became my source of food. I would silently walk to grab three or five green mangoes. That would be my supper.

This went on until in April during the holidays when I had to do some temporary work with another cousin. This was a temporary work as a garden boy, responsible for pulling weeds and taking care of the green loan as well as the beautiful flowers.

This opened a window I did not know it existed. Mr Deeds was a forty five year old white man who I worked for. He was a unique person, mainly because this was the first time I stood close to a white man. He seemed to enjoy talking to us. Sometimes we would argue with him, telling him that white people were born rich and him telling us that white people got rich because they worked very hard. We told him that it was blacks who worked hard because we had never seen whites working manually as most of the physical jobs were done by blacks, but all white families had decent lives with beautiful houses and cars while blacks lived in filthy conditions and starvation. The arguments could sometimes get so hot that my cousin could begin to raise his voice. I would start to feel my temperature rising although I kept cool and calm. I think this was due to the indoctrination we had in the bush back home. Deep in my heart, I respected Mr Deeds. He preferred to engage with me than he did with Oliver.

There were times I could feel angry in myself especially when thoughts of that white notorious soldier who broke my mother's ribs, the one who killed my uncle behind the hut as we set under the baobab tree, that who ruthlessly broke our doors with his gun. Sometimes I would start to bang the broom against the walls during cleaning time, just to annoy Mr Deeds as he would be asleep.

Mr Deeds used to be the editor with the Herald in Salisbury. He would spent the whole day at work, sometimes working overnight.

School holidays were now over, and I was about to return to school. I had no idea where I would be staying even who would pay my fees. The headmaster had warned me several times about putting on uniform. Little did he know that I had no source of money to buy uniform. I had worked for less than a month at Mr Deeds, only to be paid ten dollars. My head was a boiling pot as I pondered how to meet the school's demands, worse still, where would I be staying?

One afternoon, after a hard working day, thinking what to do, either to pack my paper bag with only my old khaki shirt and short. Surprisingly, I heard, "Dhaziiiiiii!" the voice of happiness, was followed by the door opening. Before I responded, Mr Deeds entered with a bright smile on his face. He threw a parcel he was holding on my lap and said, "There you are!" I looked at the parcel in perplex. I did not find a word. Mr Deeds went on, "That's your uniform!" I jumped high in the air with a loud voice, 'THANK YOU BAASS! THANK YOU! I stood and looked up at him and emotionally said, 'THANK YOU!' Before I cooled down, he threw an envelope and said, "And your fees!" I broke into tears. Still staring at him, happiness steered my heart. I cried calling my mother, 'Amaai! Amaai!' my voice dried out. He also dropped tears, I saw them as he looked at me with love. Both of us were in tears. He continued to say, "You will continue to stay here as you go to school and work for me during the weekends!" I stopped breathing for some seconds as I did not know what to do. I thought of hugging him, but that was not my culture, I must have briefly fainted or went into Trans due to unbelief. Never in my life had someone even my father, had done such things. With my eyes struggling to open, as tears ran down my chicks, I looked at my uniform several times. Whispering to myself. Asking how nice I would look in those grey khakis. By the time I found something to say, he had disappeared to his house. Who would I show all this? I just closed all in my heart till now as I write. To show the world how God blesses His people.

Mr Deeds opened the window of life for me. I wonder what was in his mind before he left. What I remembered was that he starred at me, shook his head and was in tears too. He was the angel sent to save me.

God had provided the whole package for me. That became my home as I continued going to school during the week, and worked for him on weekends.

Next to his house was his neighbour's house at which Jeremy worked as a house boy. Jeremy was far much older than both of us. This boy used to come to our house and walked about in Mr Deeds' house. I now suspect that he had a long hand.

One afternoon, Oliver was busy in the house as I was sieving the garden soil outside. Little did we know that our boss had called the police to arrest us.

"Hey! Young man! Come over!" the policeman called me as he stood on Mr Deeds' veranda. I hurriedly dropped everything down and timidly walked towards him. "Do you go to School?" He asked. Yes,

I am in Grade Seven Sir! I answered. "Yaa! We found the thief! You stole your Bass's $10, 00 to buy sweets at school!" The policeman harshly enquired. I was shocked at these allegations. No, I have no idea . . . . ! "Come on! Move! Your colleague is in the police van already! Jump in! You will explain in the police cell." In shock and disbelief, we set in the tight closed van. Like rats in a small cage we set, as the van veered sideways and forward. We could not tell the direction and place as we could not see outside. It took about half an hour before the van turned and parked. The doors were opened. "Come down boys!" Said the policeman. I was first, then Oliver.

They lead us to their interview rooms and asked us to stand by the desk side. One tall black policeman sat in the chair and opened a book as he asked our names one by one. He seemed to be checking in his book. After a while, he looked at us and said, "Boys! Your Boss is troublesome. We know him. Go home. Do you know how to get back home?"

"Yes Sir! Thank you Sir!" like a chorus we answered as we ran down the steps and swiftly walked out of the main gate of the Melbreign Police Station on our way back home.

As we walked down the road, we did not talk much since we were still recovering from the shock. I had no idea what Oliver was thinking, but I was thinking what would happen when we got home.

It took us an hour and half to walk home.

The drama began as soon as we entered the gate at Mr Deed's house. He was standing leaning on his stable door which was half open facing the gate.

Oliver jumped and swore at Mr Deeds as he ran towards him. "You are a Naughty Bass! Naughty Bass! Wererere! Wererere! Naughty! Bass!" By that time Mr Deeds was chasing Oliver as they ran around the house. "Oliver! Oliver! You say Naughty to Boss? Oliver!" He responded as they behaved like a rat and a cat. I was silently crying. I did not utter a word. When Mr Deeds seemed tired, he came to me. "Dhaziii! Come, let me make you a cup of tea!" Before I answered, he changed his offer and said, "Or, go and make a cup of tea for yourself. Come!" he persuaded me. 'No! Don't talk to me!' I softly declined. It was not usual those days to see a white person worse still the boss, making tea and serving a black person, it was the law of the land, in which the black person was supposed to always serve his or her master.

By that time Mr Deeds' neighbours were looking with amazement as Oliver shouted louder and louder. "You are Naughty Baass! Naughty Baass! Naughty! Wererererererere! Weeeee!" The drama went on for about half an hour or more. The two chasing each other as they went clockwise and anti-clockwise around the big house. I started to enjoy the film before I decided to engage myself.

I walked to my working area and started to sieve the garden soil as the tears dried on my chicks. Mr Deeds came to me and started to sweet talk at me, but I did not respond as I persisted with my task.

Oliver went to his room and rested. I joined him as it was already late for supper. We did not cook but just retired to bed till the following morning.

The drama above took place during the school days in October. We were just about to complete our Grade Seven examinations. I successfully wrote and passed these examinations with six points. I began to apply for a form one place at secondary school.

One bright October morning, Oliver and I woke up and set to our respective tasks. We found Mr Deeds awake standing with his hands on the stable door as usual. "Good morning Boss!" we chorus greeted him.

"Boys! I give you fourteen minutes to pack and go!" He answered.

We were dump founded. We stood and looked up at him. "Why are you looking at me? Go and pack right now!" He yelled at us.

We both turned hundred and eighty degrees and walked back into our room. There was nothing to pack. I had my paper bag with my uniform. Oliver had a suitcase in which he packed his clothes and blankets. He also had a bicycle on which he mounted his suitcase. We embarked on our journey to nowhere, Oliver in front as I followed.

Mr Deeds was still standing at the stable door. Oliver passed by, he did not say a word. I stood, turned and looked up at Mr Deeds, short as I was, I said, THANK YOU BAASS! THANK YOU! For giving me school fees, uniform and looking after me, THANK YOU! I sobbed tears of gladness and sadness. So as Mr Deeds. "Have you applied for a secondary school place yet?" He asked.

'Yes! Yes Baass! I applied at Marlborough High School,' I answered as I nodded my head.

"Keep checking for your reply because I will keep it when it comes. Good luck!" he waved at me as I did the same. His last wave was when I had just closed the gate.

I went to live with my brother Lazarus who was now working at number 64 Salisbury Drive, which today is known as 64 Harare Drive. The last time I spoke to Mr Deeds was in November 1980 when I went to his house to collect the reply to my application. He handed the letter to me with a smile, "There you are Dhaziii, but ensure not to go to expensive school." His was a wise advice as he knew well that I had not much school fees to pay. After thanks giving, I made a u-turn. That was the last time I sighted Mr Deeds.

But, what exactly took place on the Independence Day, eighteenth of April? We were in class doing a lesson in English when the final electoral results were announced. Our teacher had brought his small radio in class for that reason. The whole school went wild when it was announced that Comrade Robert Gabriel Mugabe's ZANU Party had won. The whole of the country, Zimbabwean people were in jubilation and ululation. Most Zimbabweans were satisfied as they supported this party. I cannot explain how I felt. It was as if I had gasped for the last oxygen molecule after having blocked my nose for years. The fresh air continued to flow down my nostrils into my lungs for years, until the time I escaped to diaspora.

I can confirm that today ZANU PF is no longer the popular party as it used to be. Rhodesia was renamed Zimbabwe and the capital city Salisbury became Harare. Comrade Robert Gabriel Mugabe became the first black Prime Minister of Zimbabwe as the people rejoiced at the birth of the new nation. Bob Marley and The Wailers sang the song, 'Zimbabwe' as Zimbabweans celebrated their first and hard won independence on that day, 18th of April 1980. Celebration parties were held in every corner of Zimbabwe, so was how popular comrade Robert Gabriel Mugabe and ZANU party were.

For me the struggle did not end there, as that marked the turning point towards my intense struggle for education so as to find a comfortable position in the newly born Zimbabwe. Today, I write while sitting on my chair around the table with my family here in the diaspora. It's the thirty-third year under comrade Robert Gabriel Mugabe's rule following the disputed victory in which he won by the majority against Mr Morgan Tsvangirai's Movement for Democratic Change party last July 2013.

CHAPTER SEVENTEEN

What Has Gone Wrong?

Zimbabwe! my mother, my father, my grandfather, my grandmother,
my children, my grandchildren, my land,

What has gone wrong?
When shall it be?

Your sheep have scattered all over the globe.
Running away from their shadows.
Running away from the womb of their mother.
What has gone wrong?
When shall it be?

Yesteryear, they struggled for independence.
Yesteryear they perished between the jaws of the two hot bricks.
They died and scattered in your mountains, rivers, plains and the
bushes.
Their bones, no one to burry.

What has gone wrong?
When shall it be?

They perished your children yesteryear in foreign countries, they
were buried in trenches.
In the wombs of Mozambique, South Africa, Tanzania, Kenya,
Botswana, Namibia, Zambia, Malawi no one can identify.
Today, oh! My mother!
What has gone wrong?
When shall it be?

The liberators have turned against the oppressed.
They are praying upon their eggs.
On their water they pound.
They have forgotten yesteryear they were the fish.
Oh my mother, my land!
What has gone wrong?
When shall it be?

Your sheep, moan to you day and night.
As they scatter in foreign lands.
Calling to the deaf ears of their mother.
A mother so rich in diamonds, gold, platinum, and agriculture.
A mother flowing with milk and honey.
Hear their cry!
As they long to rest their souls.
What has gone wrong?
When shall it be?

From birth your children suffered, throughout life developmental
stages they suffered.

In the tummies of baobab trees they slept.
As they ran away from jaws of the two hot bricks.
Yet today, the liberator crushes them.
In bid to silence them, he pounds on them.
What has gone wrong?

Who was he liberating?
When shall they rest?
Oh Lord my God!
What crimes did they commit?
What has gone wrong?
When shall it be?

Our Mother, our only hope, our food, our home,
We belong to you Zimbabwe,
No one can give us internal peace except you.
My mother, what has gone wrong?

Our stomachs are full, but we miss your warmth, your care, your
beautiful mountains, rivers, animals, butterflies, house flies, the
stinging wasps, and the smell of cow dungs.
Your sheep seek to rest.
What has gone wrong?
When shall it be?

Diaspora is never their mother!
Diaspora can never provide the warmth you provide.
Hear them, Oh! Lord! Hear them, Oh! My Mother!
Turn the hearts of their tormentors.
Fill them with ONE LOVE, ONE HEART and ONE
BROTHERLY LOVE.

What has gone wrong?

Your children, on their lips, continue to sing songs of war cry.
Let peace prevail in your womb.
Give them the green pastures they long for.
From you only, this shall be.
WHAT HAS GONE WRONG AGAIN?
WHEN SHALL FREEDOM BE?

"FREEDOOM! FREEDOOM! FREEDOOM!"
My mother, hear me cry!

ACKNOWLEDGEMENT

My heartfelt thanks to my beautiful wife Muchaneta, my loving children Lydia, Shingirirai, Chiedza and Shaun who unceasingly gave me courage and time to make this book a success.

Secondly but not least, my thanks to my great grandfather Changamire Chinyanda Makuni for his wisdom in passing such crucial information.

Many thanks to the great freedom fighters and their entire leadership, who fought and died to liberate our lovely nation Zimbabwe. Many thanks to comrade Vhuu and his group.